HERE'S WHAT THEY SAID ABOUT
SPENCER TRACY:

SIR LAURENCE OLIVIER: "The greatest living actor." LOUIS B. MAYER: "A troublemaker." ERNEST BORGNINE: "A wonderfully shy kind of guy." GEORGE M. COHAN: "He was brash." RICHARD WIDMARK: "Had the greatest concentration of any actor I've ever seen." ELIA KAZAN: "He's lazy." ROBERT WAGNER: "Clark Gable said to me, 'Kid, when you work with Spence, hold onto anything you can; he'll blow you away.' But he couldn't have been more kind to me." ROBERT WISE: "He couldn't have been more mean and nasty to his co-stars." GENE KELLY: "A sad, lonely guy." STANLEY KRAMER: "A raging bull." KATHARINE HEPBURN: "He was like an old lion, appearing out of the bush, glancing here, glancing there, walking alone in the jungle."

. . . AND *ALL* OF THEM WERE RIGHT!

BILL DAVIDSON

SPENCER TRACY
TRAGIC IDOL

ZEBRA BOOKS
KENSINGTON PUBLISHING CORP.

ZEBRA BOOKS

are published by

Kensington Publishing Corp.
475 Park Avenue South
New York, NY 10016

First Zebra Books printing: May, 1989

Printed in the United States of America

For my lovely Maralynne,
and the new life.

My deepest gratitude to the dozens of people who helped me with their facts, reminiscences and opinions—some very painful for them to recall.

Special thanks to Gene Kelly, Ralph Bellamy, Robert Wagner, Abby Mann and Stanley Kramer.

Chapter One

It was during the filming of *Captains Courageous* in 1937, and Spencer Tracy, as he often did, went AWOL from the Metro Goldwyn Mayer set for a couple of days. The purpose of such disappearances was well known to the studio ("his peculiar brand of alcoholism," says ex-MGM executive Eddie Lawrence); it usually involved his holing up in a hotel somewhere, drinking himself into insensibility, and then, when the binge was over, returning brilliantly to work, as if nothing had happened.

On this occasion, Tracy chose a sixth-floor room at the Beverly Wilshire Hotel, not far from the studio. As frequently happened when Tracy was on one of these solitary drinking bouts, he turned violent against inanimate objects in the room, smashing lamps and hurling furniture against the plate-glass windows. The manager of the hotel called Tracy's older brother, Carroll, the actor's closest friend and confidant. Tracy let Carroll into the locked room. The uproar continued. The manager then took the next step that was laid out for him in handling such emergencies. He phoned Howard Strickling, the powerful head of publicity at MGM.

Working for Strickling as one of many junior publicists at that time was Walter Seltzer, later the producer of such important films as *The War Lord, Darker Than Amber* and *Soylent Green*. Seltzer vividly remembers the Beverly Wilshire Hotel incident.

"It was like a wartime bombing drill which we had practised and for which we were all prepared. Strickling yelled to me, 'Get the car, and for God's sake, get Whitey.' Whitey Hendry was the head of MGM security, and for many years had been the police chief of Culver City. He had been hired for the simple reason that he had had much experience in neutralizing the peccadilloes of MGM stars so that the news of these would not get into the press.

"Half of the publicity department rushed over to the Beverly Wilshire, along with Whitey Hendry and some of his men. The nervous hotel manager opened the door to Tracy's room, to reveal an incredible sight. Tracy had his brother, Carroll, by the throat and was trying to hurl him out the sixth story window. Hendry and his men grabbed Tracy, who suddenly became docile and allowed himself to be led away. Two days later Tracy was back at work in *Captains Courageous* with the scared little English boy, Freddie Bartholomew, and he couldn't have been more kind to the 12-year-old kid, helping him with his lines, calming him down with jokes, beguiling him with stories of his own experiences on the New York stage.

"That entire incident stands out in my mind to this day because it was so typical of the enigma that was Spencer Tracy. He dearly loved his brother Carroll when he was sober, but he hated him with a violent hatred when he was drunk. He was one of the greatest actors in the world, ranked as the *best* movie actor by none other than Laurence Olivier, yet he never seemed sure of even the finest pictures he made, even walking out of some of them until he was induced to return.

"Another irony: there was one of the most beautiful Hollywood love stories in the relationship between Tracy and Katharine Hepburn — and yet, look at the tremendous ideological differences between them. He was a hidebound arch-conservative and she was a liberal much before her time. She probably was the foremost Henry Wallace Progressive Party supporter in 1948, and she was very visible in the forefront of the Wallace presidential campaign. Politically, Tracy would have been a Thomas Dewey supporter.

"Tracy's whole life seems a paradox somehow—the love for his brother and the hate for his brother; the conservative stance and the love for Hepburn; the 44-year marriage to Louise Treadwell, and the staunch Catholicism that kept him from divorcing her; his 25-year affair with Hepburn which flaunted the rules of the Church. There were a lot of very interesting contradictory positions in Mr Tracy."

Enigma.

He could be cruel and heartless toward some actors with whom he worked; overwhelmingly kind to others. Director Robert Wise says, "When we did a film called *Tribute to a Bad Man,* which he never finished because I fired him, he couldn't have been more mean and nasty to his co-stars. He derided Irene Papas because she was too tall, too clumsy, and her English didn't suit him because she was from Greece. He ignored and upstaged young Robert Francis to the point where the kid, who was so good in *The Caine Mutiny,* was hurt, bewildered and demoralized."

On the other hand, Robert Wagner says, "After I worked with Spence in *The Mountain* in 1955, he became sort of a surrogate father to me. We became good friends and he helped me in my development as an actor until the day he died."

Van Johnson actually gives Tracy credit for his entire career. He once told me,

"When I was a kid at Metro Goldwyn Mayer, I used to watch Spence work every spare minute I had. Then came the big moment of my life when I was assigned to do *A Guy Named Joe* with Tracy and Irene Dunne. Then, when I was nearly killed in a motorcycle accident—my scalp was torn away—Spence went to one of the top studio executives, Benny Thau, and insisted that the studio hold up production until I could return. Thau gave in, although he simply wanted to replace me with another young actor. They waited for me, costing the studio a lot of money, until I was well enough to work. Without Tracy, my career could have ended then and there. He never was anything but kind and helpful to me, and he saw to it that we worked together again in a lot of other pictures."

There was a similar dichotomy in Tracy's relations with directors. He got along well with some, John Sturges and Stanley Kramer, for example, but even Kramer says, "There were times, when he disagreed with me, when he could wither me with a glance. If his forehead was shiny, and I sent a makeup man over to powder-puff it, he'd push the man away and give him a look as though he were something he had just thrown up."

These were comparatively mild reactions, and generally he went along with everything a director wanted. But with the highly respected Walter Lang, Tracy was downright rude. Before production began on *Desk Set,* Lang asked Tracy for a get-together conference—not an unusual request for a director to make of an actor with whom he had not worked before. Tracy's reply: "Go screw yourself. If you want to know what I look like, I'm gray and I'm fat!"

More Tracy paradox: when he discovered that his son, John, had been born deaf, Tracy was traumatized. Said his friend, Pat O'Brien, in a 1961 interview with me,

"Spence felt less a man and lost his self-esteem, because, in our Irish Catholic culture, your sperm doesn't produce an imperfect child. It was not known in those days that such things can happen if the mother has German measles during pregnancy. Yet, when the initial shock wore off, no one could have lavished more love on the boy. And when Louise Tracy founded the John Tracy Clinic to help their deaf son, and other deaf children, and the parents of other deaf children, Spence never turned down a request to make appearances in fundraising for the clinic."

There are varying opinions even within the un-contested view that Tracy was among the great actors of all time. Angela Lansbury, who appeared with him in the film *State of the Union,* says, "His greatness as an actor had a lot to do with his own persona. He had an extraordinary understanding of the common man, which he was, and which he always played. He never played the aristocrat. He understood that person he enacted, had a brilliant knowledge of all his reactions—and never let his own personal demons intrude on the character."

Richard Widmark agrees, but adds an interesting footnote. "When I worked with Spence in *Judgment at Nuremberg,* my feeling was that his talent was so finely tuned that it was almost too easy for him. I know that Laurence Olivier always was trying to get Spence to play more challenging things, Shakespeare for instance, and what a King Lear he would have been. But Spence always poo-poohed the idea, saying 'I'm happy with what I'm doing.' "

I know that Elia Kazan understood this underly-ing attitude of Spence's when he directed him in *Sea of Grass.* Never one to mince words, Kazan said of Spence, "He's lazy."

And so the contradictions and the complications continue. They even extend to his relationship with Katharine Hepburn. Gene Kelly says, "It was the most exciting and heartwarming thing to watch them at Metro. Katie would be working in one picture and Spence in another and at lunchtime they'd just meet and sit on a bench on the lot. They'd hold hands and talk — and everybody left them alone in their little private world. We all could sense and feel that they were exuding love."

Stanley Kramer, on the other hand, reports that while their love was real and deep and pervasive, Tracy could sometimes be mean to Hepburn. Kramer says that when they worked together, Tracy frequently became impatient with Kate's intellectual approach to acting — wanting to know the meaning of what she saw in the script. Says Kramer, "Spence would bellow at her, 'Goddamit, Katie, just read the lines the writer wrote and do what Stanley tells you to do.' Spence also was intolerant of her upper-class Eastern accent. He used to say, 'Goddamit, Kate, why do you always talk like you've got a feather up your ass?' "

Why the contradictions? Why the sudden mood changes from affection to intolerance, from love to hate, from affability to cantankerousness, from intense pride-of-craft to laziness? Ralph Bellamy, one of Tracy's closest friends and protectors in the old days, says, "Spence was an alcoholic. That's the answer to everything. He was an alcoholic who knew it and fought it. He deserves credit for that, even though he didn't always win the fight."

And so we come to the underlying tragedy of the man. In Tracy's day, alcoholism was thought of as a mostly amusing social aberration, not as a medical problem; as a disease. Alcoholics Anonymous was coming into existence, but it was unheard of for a studio to allow one of its major stars to risk public exposure by attending AA meetings. So the most that was done was attempted "therapy" by ineffectual studio-trusted physicians (many of them untreated alcoholics themselves) plus periods of "drying out" in secret spas, sanatoriums and selected hospitals, where booze was readily available to any sly and well-heeled patient, thus causing the "cure" to abet rather than cure the problem.

How different from today, when stars can come out of the closet and openly seek help at chemical dependency centres like the Betty Ford Institute at Long Beach (California) Naval Base. Alcohol, cocaine, heroin, any other addictive chemical, it makes no difference. With proper guidance, the patients are given a *chance*. Today, aided by the proper therapy to begin their recovery, many make it out of dependency.

But Tracy and others of his generation had to try to do it on their own, "the white-knuckle way," as AA puts it, and it hardly ever worked.

Tracy *did* try, and thus commands our compassion and understanding, rather than our condemnation. Unlike public carousers, like John Barrymore and Errol Flynn, he mostly did his drinking in private. Except for a few occasions, he was always totally professional on a set or location, and did not allow his drinking urges to interfere with his work. His technique, as an alcoholic, was to go on periodic binges and not show up for work. As he once told me, "Anyone who stayed drunk for twenty-five years, as I did, would have to be in trouble. Hell, I used to take two-week lunch hours. Sometimes I'd get on a train and go to another city until I had drunk myself out."

Ex-MGM executive Eddie Lawrence is one of the few to disagree with the premise that Tracy was always sober on the set:

"He was the kind of alcoholic who could take one drink and he was gone. He fell asleep a lot during filming. On *Tortilla Flat,* he was supposed to say a line while he was cutting squid, and he just couldn't manage to get the line right. In the next line, a priest says to him, 'It must have been something you drank, my son.' Tracy broke up so that he couldn't work the rest of the day."

No one knows Tracy's struggle against the bottle better than Ralph Bellamy. Nor the depths of degradation to which Tracy was capable of falling.

"When we both were at Fox, I could always sense when one of Spence's binges would be coming on. He'd get even more mean and cantankerous than he usually was. Then he'd

16

suddenly disappear. A few days later, he'd show up on my doorstep, usually in the middle of the night. He'd look like a bum on Skid Row, smelly, dirty and with a growth of stubble on his face. He always wore a heavy overcoat, even in ninety-degree weather. Every pocket of the coat was crammed with whisky bottles. If he'd say, 'How about some scrambled eggs and bacon?' I'd know he was all right.

"I'd take him inside and feed him the bacon and eggs. Then he'd sleep it off in my house, clean himself up, go home in some clothes he borrowed from me, and he'd be ready to go back to work—until the next time. He'd always be overcome with remorse, and he'd try desperately to keep it from happening again. But it kept happening. What a pity there wasn't the proper kind of help for him in those days."

1986 was the year of the deification of Spencer Tracy, who had died nineteen years before, in 1967. Katharine Hepburn narrated a film for the Public Broadcasting System entitled *The Spencer Tracy Legacy: A Tribute by Katharine Hepburn*. Other Tracy encomia appeared on cable television. The American Academy of Dramatic Arts staged a live tribute at the Majestic Theater in New York and filled the house, with seats ranging in price up to five hundred dollars. Tracy's daughter, Susie, accepted a lifetime achievement award on her father's behalf, and a Spencer Tracy Endowment Fund was established for student scholarships.

All of these tributes emphasized Tracy's greatness as an actor, and rightly so, but the dark and troubled side of the man was barely mentioned.

How much more meaningful and dramatic the Tracy tributes would have been if the public had been allowed to glimpse the struggle, the courage, the achieving of greatness, *despite* the crippling disease which sapped him.

Chapter Two

Having relived Tracy's life through observation and research, certain images of the man remain with me:

Tracy and fellow-Milwaukeean Pat O'Brien are struggling young actors in New York. The sanctity of the Broadway stage is inviolable to them, but Hollywood is doing its recruitment along the Great White Way, and the temptations are beginning. O'Brien is one of the tempted. A man from United Artists has been around to see him several times. Tracy says, "If you go out there, you'll get to be just like everybody else in the movies. You'll lose the individuality that makes you a good actor." O'Brien says, "Never. If anything, I'll help change them." Rejoins Tracy "Yeah. That's what the cucumber said just before they threw it into the pickle barrel."

The line was later attributed to Oscar Le-

vant, in a similar conversation with George Gershwin. But O'Brien swore to me that Tracy said it first.

Image: it's on the sweltering set of The Devil at Four O'Clock *in Hawaii in 1961. Tracy is furious. A reporter has been allowed on the location to interview him without his previous authorization. He is chewing out Bob Yeager, the Columbia Pictures press agent, a quiet and funny man. Yeager interrupts Tracy's tirade by saying, mildly, "Mr Tracy, you shouldn't be yelling at me. You should be yelling at my bosses in Public Relations back in Hollywood. I am nothing but a caraway seed in the bakery of life." Tracy, a great appreciator of the* bon mot, *forgets his tirade and laughs so hard that he gets diarrhoea.*

Image: it's the crucial scene in Bad Day at Black Rock, *when Tracy first walks into the bar and is confronted by the hostile townspeople who don't want him around to look into the disappearance of a Japanese farmer to whom he wants to give a medal. In the scene, the then very young Lee Marvin keeps flipping the lid of a match book while he is sitting at the bar. Tracy stops the action, and walks up to Marvin, saying, "Young man, I'm too old, and too experienced, and I've been around too long for you to be pulling attention-grabbing tricks like that on me." Marvin stops flipping the match book.*

Image: the great photographer Phil Stern has been sent to Paris to photograph Tracy on the roof of his hotel for a promotion poster for Judgment at Nuremberg. *Tracy keeps walking over to the edge of the roof to look down into the street below. "Looking for Kate," he explains to Stern. "She's supposed to be coming here to the hotel." He becomes more and more distraught, and Stern becomes more and more puzzled.*

"But why are you looking down at the back of the hotel instead of at the front entrance?" Stern finally asks.

"Kate always *comes in the back way," says Tracy. "Gotta be discreet, ya know."*

Fleeting images, captured like fireflies, because Tracy was a man whom very few people ever really knew. A loner who flitted in and out of friendships from the time he was a youth, he was the epitome of today's cliché, "he's a very private person." Clark Gable, when filming his last picture, *The Misfits,* once spoke to me with puzzlement about his long-time MGM co-star.

"Spence? I got as close to him as anybody could. God knows, we did a lot of drinking together, and when a guy boozes with a friend, he usually lets his hair down and lets

21

you know something about what's going on inside his noggin. But not Spence. It was like he had a curtain in there. He was a guy with a lot of things bothering him, but he never lifted that curtain to let me know what was buggin' him."

Similarly, the late Humphrey Bogart told me, "Spence was a great story-teller and a great guy, but when it came to personal things, he always changed the subject."

Claudette Colbert was among dozens of actresses I interviewed who worked in films with Tracy (Colbert was in *Boom Town*), but never got to know him off-camera, and could say nothing about the inner workings of this complex, troubled, brilliant man.

Not even Katharine Hepburn, after twenty-five years of intimate relationship. In a touching personal letter to Tracy, which she read in the 1986 Public Broadcasting System tribute, *The Spencer Tracy Legacy*, she plaintively asked her long-dead companion, "Are you happy, finally? Is it a nice long rest you're having, making up for all your tossing and turning in life? Why, Spence? Why could you not sleep? I still wonder. Living wasn't easy for you, was it?"

It was not. And maybe the roots of all that unease, all that restlessness and self-destructiveness, can be found in the childhood and early years of

Spencer Tracy, in the first decades of the twentieth century.

Tracy was born in Milwaukee on 5 April 1900, into a family which had conflict built in. His father, John, was a devout, hard-driving, Irish Catholic businessman (he was general sales manager of the old Sterling Motor Truck Company), who, according to the legend later imparted to Spencer, went out and got drunk in all of Milwaukee's Irish bars ("free drinks for all") on the night of his son's nativity. Spencer's mother, on the other hand, was the gentle, well-born Carrie, a descendant of the colonial-period Browns of New England, one of whom founded the Ivy League Brown University in Providence, Rhode Island. A Protestant (later a Christian Scientist), Carrie called in the hospital chaplain and gave quiet thanks to God while her husband was out making the rounds of the saloons.

One cannot presume that these religious differences had any effect on Spencer's early childhood because, as his older brother Carroll once told me,

> "Dad was a tough, decisive, no-nonsense man, and there never was any doubt that we'd be raised as Catholics. When we were old enough, Spence and I both became altar boys. Later, in the Catholic schools, Spence got very

interested in the theology of the Church. One of dad's greatest hopes was that one of us would become a priest. We both disappointed him. His second hope was that, if neither of us went into the Church, he'd be able to form a trucking company with us which he'd call Tracy and Sons. Again, we disappointed him. I think Spence carried a lot of guilt around about disappointing Dad. Spence was more mother's favorite, and I was Dad's, and I always figured Spence was in a constant battle with himself to win Dad over."

Whatever the reasons, and there was no psychiatrist in Tracy's life, then or later, to pinpoint them, the young Spencer Tracy evolved into what would be called, today, a disturbed child. Neither he nor anyone else, to all outward appearances, anyway, ever recognized that fact. In all earlier writings, he was always portrayed as a rebellious, mischievous child who did a lot of fist-fighting with other boys, but was no more abnormal than, say, Huckleberry Finn. In 1937, Tracy wrote "My Life Story," a series of articles for the *Milwaukee Sentinel,* employing the florid, cliché-ridden journalistic style of the day, which indicated that he was probably abetted in this endeavour by an MGM press agent.

In the articles, he wrote of himself as the typical tough Irish kid in an urban working-class society. He was fun-loving, adventurous, and normally combative in an ethnically-mixed German, Polish and Irish community. A few darker clues slip through, however, in Tracy's autobiographical ramblings. He tells, for example, how he once set fire to his family's house. Also, he casually mentions that "I attended maybe fifteen to eighteen grammar schools before I finally graduated."

Fifteen schools to complete eight grades? The records indicate that he was withdrawn from some of the schools by his parents, but mostly he was expelled for constant truancy and for being a disruptive influence by way of habitual fighting with other students. And how about the fire in his home? It is passed off as a typical childish accident, resulting from mischievous experimentation with cigarettes in the basement. However, a neighbor, Margaret Foley, recalled, "The boy had a screaming and yelling fight with his father that day, and then he went down into the cellar. It was a big fire, lots of paper and wood-shavings and all. The Fire Department had to be called and it took them a good twenty minutes to put it out. It was a Sunday morning, after church, as I remember. The mother, Carrie, told the firemen it was the boy playing with matches and cigarettes. They said, 'OK, then, if you vouch for it,' and they went away."

Tracy's childhood was not poverty-stricken, as some 1940s magazine articles would lead you to believe. The father, John Tracy, was a good provider, although he seems to have been an impulsive, chance-taking businessman who had occasional economic ups and downs. The family first lived in a house with a veranda and slate roof, on Prospect Avenue, just a block from Lake Michigan, and one of the better neighborhoods in town. It still is a fine neighborhood, as I discovered on a recent trip to Milwaukee. The Tracy house is gone, but Prospect Avenue is a street of expensive condominiums, old mansions converted into offices for lawyers, an eye clinic, a music conservatory, and such.

When Spencer grew up there, most of the wealthy Irish lived in Shorewood, to the north; the poorer Irish lived to the west and south, in neighborhoods like the rough-and-tumble Tory Hill. Spencer used to journey on foot and by trolley car to both areas, and generally ended up in fights. It is not known why he liked to pick fights with his fellow Irish, but a friend and neighbor, Forrest McNicol, once indicated that Tracy was an equal-opportunity belligerent and did not discriminate among Irish, Germans, Poles or Italians.

Many of Tracy's fights apparently came about because of his aversion to school, while he restlessly wandered the city while playing truant. He himself mentions one of the earlier episodes in his *Milwaukee Sentinel* autobiographical series. He was only seven years old, and about to start the second grade. He had heard rumors that the teacher was a tough disciplinarian, and therefore he did not want to even *start* the second grade. He was locked in his room by his irate father, but managed to escape through a window and down a drainpipe. He had decided to run away from home.

Young Tracy meandered all the way to the South Side where, eventually, he found himself outside Donovan's Saloon. He encountered Donovan's two sons, nicknamed Mousy and Ratty, playing on the street in front of the saloon. The inevitable fist fight ensued, with Spencer taking on Ratty, the older brother, who was about the same age and size. The fight ended in a draw, whereupon the three kids began playing together. The Donovan children, apparently, were not required to go to school by their bar-keeper father, and compulsory education was not rigidly enforced in 1907.

In the meantime, back on Prospect Avenue, Carrie Tracy became distraught when she discovered her son's absence. She went to the school to find Carroll, whose primary duty seemed to be to keep an eye on his miscreant younger brother, but Carroll, of course, knew nothing about where Spencer might be. Mrs. Tracy then rounded up her husband John, and they began scouring the city for their missing son. Back at the saloon, Donovan finally began to worry about the strange well-dressed boy playing outside with his sons. He notified the police who notified the Tracys who rushed over to the South Side saloon.

27

As Carroll Tracy later recalled it, "My father yelled. My mother cried. Spence promised that he'd never make Mom cry again, and that he'd start the second grade—which he did, for a while."

There was some improvement in Spence as he grew older. He joined the Boy Scouts, became an altar boy, and transferred some of his kinetic energy to the baseball field and to gym boxing, at both of which he was very good.

But the school truancies and the school expulsions continued, and so did his sudden disappearances. He used to agonize his mother by wandering over to the Kinnickinnick River mud flats, a hangout for derelicts. For many years, his best friends continued to be Mousy and Ratty Donovan. When school got to be too much of a trial for him, young Tracy would take the long journey on foot to the saloon, to renew his relationship with Mousy and, especially, Ratty (of whom he later wrote in his *Milwaukee Sentinel* articles, "Ratty turned out pretty well. The last I heard, he was a successful financier on Wall Street"). He also wrote that he and Ratty used to hide under the bar in the saloon, listening to the earthy chatter of the customers. Tracy's brother, Carroll, told me he suspected that Spencer, at the age of ten, began sampling the drippings from the draught-beer mechanism, as he huddled with Ratty under the Donovan bar.

Another random image of the adult Tracy:

In 1967, Buck Herzog, Milwaukee's most celebrated local columnist, wrote in the *Sentinel:*

"Spencer Tracy made many secret visits to his native Milwaukee during his celebrated career. I know. At the end of a picture assignment, he would take off with his brother Carroll for a little relaxation. Many times, Carroll or the late Eugene Sullivan, a relative by marriage, alerted me that Tracy was coming to town or had sneaked into the city. Then we'd meet at Sam Pick's Club Madrid for a festive night, and wind up in the wee hours of the morning.

"In 1944, when Tracy officiated at the launching of a submarine in Manitowoc, I received a call from Carroll that he and his brother would be arriving at the Pfister Hotel the next day. He asked that I keep the news quiet until after they left. Apparently Tracy trusted my security measures.

"Spencer was drinking scotch and milk then and, during his several days stay, the great number of empty milk bottles left in the suite were evidence of his ulcerated condition.

"He entered a Chicago hospital the day after he left for treatment of his ulcers."

Chapter Three

At a time which is difficult to pinpoint, but probably around 1912, John Tracy suffered one of his financial reverses, and the family moved to a far less-affluent area than Prospect Avenue. The new home was on the West Side, at the corner of St. Paul Avenue and 30th Street. It was a mostly Irish neighborhood then, as it still is, with neat little houses on a knoll overlooking the industrial Menominee River Valley. In the valley below, there are factories, a burial casket company, a slaughter house and railroad yards. In the young Tracy's day, the workers could walk to work from their homes on the knoll.

For some reason, Spencer's aberrant behaviour seemed to improve with the change in environment. Perhaps, with his penchant for the common man, as later expressed so eloquently by Angela Lansbury, he felt more at home with the kids of St. Paul Avenue than he did with the children of the well-to-do on Prospect Avenue. The new kids were more like Mousy and Ratty.

Still, the fights continued. Some of the fights took place because Spencer now had become an aficionado of the silent movies then playing in the local Bijou, and he put on shows in the basement of his new house. The shows were live, written by Spencer on the basis of what he had seen on the silver screen. His customers were charged one cent, and occasionally there were mini-riots over the quality of the scripts, and over the fact that Spencer hogged most of the good parts for himself. Brother Carroll reported that he spent a good deal of time serving as Spencer's bodyguard during these mêlées. Carroll said, "Spence could handle himself with two or three kids, but when there were five or six swinging at him, he was in trouble. At eighteen, I was four years older than most of them and big enough to be a peacekeeper."

Spencer still loathed school. He once said, "The only reason I went was so I could read the sub-titles in the silent movies." Actually, the only reason he went was because of the beatings and threats from his father, and the tearful entreaties of his mother. From the age of twelve on, he really wanted to go out and get a job in the factories or railroad yards of Menominee Valley, which was possible in those days before child labor laws. But, because of the threats and entreaties, he transferred to yet another school — his fifteenth or sixteenth. This was St. Rose's, a Catholic parochial school, just one block from the Tracy's new home on St. Paul Avenue.

St. Rose's provides another interesting episode in the tumultuous saga of this strange child. He liked it. His truancies diminished, although they did not cease completely. He was not so prone to provoke fights, and he actually became a fairly good student for the first time in his life. What brought about the metamorphosis? He had been to parochial schools before, but, at this stage of his development, according to brother Carroll, Spencer seemed to enjoy the religiousness, the kindness and understanding of these particular nuns at St. Rose's.

But there may be another more basic factor involved. Remembering John Tracy's ambitions for his son to become a priest, and Spencer's indifference to the idea, one could theorize that the St. Rose's experience was an attempt to please and placate his father; to win his love and respect; to indicate to him that he might yet be drawn to enter the priesthood.

In any event, Spencer actually graduated from St. Rose's with his eighth-grade diploma. Some accounts say he was at the very head of his class, but there are no records to support that assertion. What is true is that, because of all his previous school-changes and expulsions, he was older and bigger than his fellow graduates. This age-factor was to plague Tracy, and make him uncomfortable throughout the rest of his educational experience.

Then, after St. Rose's came a major disruption in Spencer's life, and a return to the old ways. His father was offered a good business deal in Kansas City, and the family abruptly packed up and moved. Kansas City was a dismal interlude for Spencer. He was sixteen at the time and entered St. Mary's High School, another Catholic institution, but he did not react to it as he had to St. Rose's. He resumed his fist fights with other students and, quite literally, got kicked out after just a few weeks of attendance. He then went to Rockhurst High, a secular school, but it was no different there. There were more fights, and, this time, a near-fight with a teacher. By now, Tracy, with his blue eyes and thick reddish hair was finding himself attractive to girls, and them to him. However, his first dates were disastrous, with one young lady so resenting his bellicose attitude that she threw a punch at *him*.

He was just about to be expelled from Rockhurst, when, to his relief, his father's business venture failed, and the family returned to Milwaukee just six months after they left it. They moved into an apartment near the old Prospect Avenue neighbourhood. Once again, there was a Catholic school for Spencer, this time a very good one, in fact one of the best in the country. It was Marquette Academy, a Jesuit-run high school associated with Marquette University in Milwaukee.

Tracy's introduction and admission to Marquette Academy came about in a circuitous way. About two years earlier, during his wanderings in the Tory Hill neighbourhood of Milwaukee, he had come across a glib, dark-haired boy named Bill O'Brien who was several months older and seemed highly sophisticated to Spence. The boy was later to change his name to Pat O'Brien, and was already interested in becoming an actor. Spencer, at the time, thought acting was an effeminate profession for a tough kid from Milwaukee, but, because of his own interest in movies, he listened with fascination to O'Brien's somewhat embellished tales (gleaned from reading *Vanity Fair*) of the lives of George M. Cohan, the Barrymores, *et al* on the New York stage.

Upon his return to Milwaukee from Kansas City, Spencer renewed his friendship with O'Brien. In hunting him down, he discovered that O'Brien was in school, on a scholarship from the Ancient Order of Hibernians, at Marquette Academy. After visiting O'Brien a couple of times at the Academy, Spencer decided that he wanted to go there, too. It was an easy sell to his parents, although the cost of tuition was steep. He later told me, "They were so intrigued that I wanted to go to *any* school, that I think they might even have said OK to a Jewish *yeshiva*."

To the surprise and delight of John Tracy, Spence became heavily involved in the Catholic

35

theology courses at Marquette Academy, and brought home the highest grades in the subject that his father had ever seen his young son attain. Not only that, but Spencer began talking seriously for the first time about becoming a priest. John Tracy was ecstatic.

But, once again, a major disruption in Spence's life interrupted what now seemed to be a clear path into a career in the Church. The disruption was the sinking of the *Lusitania* and America's entry into World War I. Being considerably older than his sophomore classmates at the Academy, Spence felt it his patriotic duty to go to downtown Milwaukee and enlist in the Marine Corps. He was turned down because of his age; he was not yet eighteen. He then learned from O'Brien, that *he* had been accepted in the Navy at the age of seventeen, provided his parents would consent. So Spencer went home and discussed it with his father and mother, to the accompaniment of the usual teeth-gnashing and weeping. They finally said yes when brother Carroll indicated that he would enlist, too, to keep an eye on baby brother.

So Spencer, Carroll and O'Brien all trooped off to war which, in their case, happened to be the Great Lakes Naval Training Station, about eighty-five miles away, in the Chicago area. The war was a bombshell for all of them—mostly guard duty and pot-scrubbing. It was the same when Spencer was transferred to the Norfolk Navy Yard in Virginia. He scrubbed down ships and toilets, and spent long lonely hours on watch. "Over there" and the fight against the Kaiser were just as far away as they had been in Milwaukee. The closest Tracy came to being on a moving ship was when he rode whaleboats in the harbour.

In his seven months at Norfolk, Seaman Tracy was remembered by a man in his unit, Stanley Fischer, as "a guy who kept to himself and brooded a lot." Said Fischer, "Once in a while he'd go out in Norfolk with the rest of us guys on liberty, but what I remember about him was that he couldn't hold his liquor. A few beers and he'd pass out, and we'd have to lug him back to his bunk. He wanted girls, like the rest of us, but he never made it because he couldn't stay sober enough."

What was he brooding about? He later told writer J. P. McEvoy that he thought a lot about how much he had disappointed his parents "and had to get his life in order."

Yet, when he was discharged from the Navy, soon after the Armistice in November 1918, he proceeded to disappoint his father again by returning to Marquette Academy with his interest in becoming a Catholic priest now wholly dissipated. A 19-year-old junior among 16-year-old classmates, he felt out of place. The same circumstance did not seem to bother Pat O'Brien who joined the school's ROTC unit, played quarterback on the varsity football team, wore his Seaman Second Class uniform to all classes, and then stubbornly insisted on graduating in it. *He* was having a great time. He still talked incessantly about the theatre and had actually performed in a play, an amateur production of *The Prince and the Pauper.* His prattlings about the stage finally got to the otherwise listless Tracy who spent the summer of 1919 going to see most of the touring stage productions that passed through Milwaukee.

Nonetheless, Spencer abruptly left Marquette Academy and his friend, O'Brien, behind, and enrolled, for no explainable reason, in the Northwestern Military and Naval Academy at Lake Geneva, Wisconsin. "I don't know," said O'Brien. "Spence had been talking about being a priest, a doctor, a lawyer, an actor. Maybe he was confused and wanted to get back to the kind of life he had in the Navy where he didn't have to think much about what he was going to do, or fight with his parents about it any more."

Tracy's senior high-school year at Northwestern Academy was undistinguished. Once again he found himself uncomfortable, at nearly twenty, with a cadet corps that was mostly three or four years younger. The best thing that happened to Spencer in that year was that he was assigned a room-mate, 17-year-old Kenneth Edgers, a cultured, sophisticated boy from Seattle, who was later to become a dentist. Edgers had a great influence on the young Tracy. Because he was determined to go on to Ripon, one of the best small colleges in the Midwest, Tracy, the follower, decided to go to Ripon, too.

It was there after so many wanderings, that the previously aimless youth finally found his calling. But it was not the calling that John Tracy, his father, had been hoping for.

Chapter Four

Ripon is a charming little campus near Fond du Lac, Wisconsin, in the lake country about a hundred miles to the north and west of Milwaukee. It was a rich kids' school when Tracy matriculated there on 11 January 1921. Ordinarily, his poor high-school grades would not have been good enough to get him in, but America was still in post-World War I patriotic fervour and veterans—even those who never got beyond Norfolk Harbour—were welcome in all institutions of higher learning. The Government paid thirty dollars a month toward their tuition, which was usually enough in those days.

Once again, Tracy roomed with Kenneth Edgers. Once again, he was older and more mature-looking than the other freshmen, a fact which drew the attention of Professor J. Clark Graham, who ran a one-man drama department and continuously despaired about having to put on plays with callow youths in mature, manly parts.

Professor Graham invited Tracy to try out for the annual spring school play which was only a couple of months off.

The play was to be *The Truth,* by Clyde Fitch, a fairly well-known playwright of the period. Tracy tried out. With many of the other male-lead aspirants still struggling with change-of-voice problems, Tracy's resonant manner of speaking stood out. Professor Graham also was impressed with an attribute which was to be a Tracy hallmark for the rest of his life. He had a fantastic memory, and, even at twenty-one, he had memorized the script of *The Truth* to the point that he, and no one else, auditioned without a script in his hand.

Needless to say, he got the male-lead part. As *College Days,* the campus newspaper reported on 17 March 1921, "Spencer Tracy is chosen to play the role of Warder in *The Truth,* commencement play. Tracy is new to the Ripon stage, but should prove to be one of the strongest actors in the cast, if the ability revealed last Tuesday may be taken as a sample of his future work."

On 23 June 1921, the day after the play was performed, *College Days* pronounced the production a hit, "One of the best in the proud history of Ripon Drama." Concerning the newcomer-star, the paper wrote, "Mr Tracy proved himself a consistent and unusually strong actor in this most difficult straight part. His steadiness, his reserve strength and suppressed emotion were a pleasant surprise to all who heard him as Warder."

Considering that, unlike Pat O'Brien, say, this was the first time in his life that Tracy had ever set foot on a theatrical stage, his initial Ripon College accomplishment was indicative of his great *instinctive* acting talents, another quality that characterized his later years.

He became enthralled with the theatre and with Professor Graham, who provided Tracy with lists of books he should read about drama. He did not do well in his other courses, however. He was a poor student in Professor H. P. Boody's literature course, for example, and ended the first semester with barely passing grades overall. He didn't say much to his parents about his acting triumph in *The Truth*. During a brief visit to Milwaukee, on his way to spend the summer with his room-mate, Kenneth Edgers, in the Northwest, he told his father, "I think I want to be a doctor now."

When the autumn semester began at Ripon, Tracy was induced to take a public-speaking course with the same Professor Boody who had not been thrilled with the young man in English literature. To impress Boody, and to exploit his new-found acting talents, Tracy overwhelmed the public-speaking class with an impromptu monologue about his sister, who had died after leading a short and unhappy life. He, of course, never had a sister, but his recitation had the class in tears. He had won Boody over.

43

He won the professor over even more when he played the lead in Professor Graham's fall production, *The Valiant,* which bestirred the campus paper, *College Days,* to exult, on 1 November 1921: "Spencer Tracy, who scored a hit last June in *The Truth,* played the part of a doomed prisoner in *The Valiant* so well that his audience felt with him the emotions he portrayed. His was the part of a bravado controlling his emotions and hiding his identity."

Whatever *that* means, Professor Boody, once so cynical about Tracy, was now really impressed. He invited him to join the varsity debating team, of which he was the faculty adviser. With Tracy's forceful voice, and uncanny ability to memorize printed material on any subject, he became the middle man between two experienced debaters, Harold Bumby and Curtis MacDougall. Boody named this three-man team to represent Ripon in an Eastern tour against such intercollegiate opponents as Bowdoin, Northwestern and Illinois Wesleyan.

But Tracy had something else on his mind. Apparently he was planning to use the debating tour, scheduled for February 1922, as a means of getting him to where he wanted to go. On 6 December 1921, he had starred in another play at Ripon, *The Great Divide,* and then, over the Christmas holiday, had gone on a tour of small Wisconsin towns with the Campus Players of Ripon, redoing his

44

previous triumph, *The Truth*. Wrote the college newspaper about one stop on this tour: "We found one of the best hotels in Wautome and one of the best theaters. We overheard this remark which was made to Tracy: 'I saw this play in the movies once and I think you imitated them real swell.'"

All of which had impelled Professor Graham, the drama teacher, to write to the American Academy of Dramatic Arts in New York, suggesting that they give Tracy a tryout, should he ever come to the city. Tracy knew that the debating-team tour would take him to New York for three days, which is why, apparently, he was so interested in debating in the midst of all this theatre activity. His father, not too enthralled with his son's acting, liked the idea of his son's skill at debating, attributing it to his Jesuitical training at Marquette Academy. He still had not given up on the idea of his son eventually becoming a priest.

The Ripon debating team headed east on 22 February 1922. They beat Illinois Wesleyan, tied Northwestern and lost to Bowdoin. Tracy did well as the middle man in these debates, but he was far more interested in the professional theatres he was able to attend en route. In his diary, he noted that Laurette Taylor, in *Peg 0' My Heart,* and Lionel Barrymore, in *The Claw,* were the best actors he had ever seen because of "their naturalness in making me believe what they were supposed to be."

Then came the long-awaited three days in New

York with the debating team. Leaving his fellow debaters at their hotel, Tracy nervously made his way to the American Academy of Dramatic Arts in the Carnegie Hall building. To his amazement, the founder of the Academy in 1884, Franklin Havens Sargent, was waiting for him in a small theatre he used as his office.

Sargent asked Tracy if he had brought any dramatic material to read to him, and Tracy replied that, indeed, he had come with a one-act play he had memorized. Sargent knew the play, *Sintram of Sgagerrak,* and said, "OK, I'll read the other part with you." Having heard Tracy read, Sargent said, "All right, young man. You can start with us in June, earlier if you want to." The flabbergasted Tracy mumbled his thanks and ran out. Sargent later said of this interview, "I took to the boy because he was manly and was capable of a strong, dominating presence. It just so happened that, on that very morning, I had been worrying about how many effeminate or too-pretty actors were flocking into the theater. This boy certainly wasn't pretty, and I thought of him as part of a much-needed change in the Academy's admission policies."

Tracy rushed back to Ripon campus with his two fellow debaters. They were hailed as heroes for their .500 record against larger colleges. Harold Bumby knew about Tracy's interview at the Dramatic Arts Academy and was puzzled at Tracy's apparent depression. Said Bumby later, "Spencer became more withdrawn than usual, and he *always* was a difficult guy to know." What happened was that Tracy anticipated an outraged howl from his father at the news that he was planning to leave college to study acting full-time. But the howl never came from John Tracy; in fact, he was surprisingly supportive. Perhaps he had given up trying to guide the life of his mercurial son.

As sensitive as Spencer was to his father's ambitions for him, he doubtlessly suffered some guilt over his decision to start at the Academy in New York as soon as possible, not even waiting until June.

Other guilts followed. Ripon and Professor Graham had been so instrumental in helping him find the profession he felt he was best suited for. Tryouts for the spring campus play were just beginning, and he was counted on to be the male lead again. And yet, without ceremony, he quietly informed a few students he was leaving and then slipped away.

The date was 11 April 1922. He had been at Ripon College exactly one year and eighty-nine days. "I was running away again," he later wrote.

Another Tracy image from later in life:

It's 10 June 1940. Tracy has been called back to Ripon College to receive the honorary degree of Doctor of Dramatic Art. He arrives with an MGM executive, Frank Whitbeck, to make sure he doesn't go astray. Professor Graham is now the Dean and speaks of Tracy's two Academy Awards "and the great promise you showed in your college days." Professor Boody says, "I am finishing twenty-five years of teaching here and the friendship and loyalty of this former student has been one of my greatest joys." Tracy mumbles, "God bless you all and give you strength to carry on."

No one mentions Tracy's abrupt departure on 11 April 1922, or the fact that he had finished just a little more than his freshman year at Ripon.

Chapter Five

Tracy arrived in New York on 16 April 1922, after sitting up all night on a gruelling train ride from Chicago. Like all young actors, he was filled with hope and anticipation, but it was to be another seven years before he finally made it *really* big in the theatre.

His initial hardships in the Big City have been amply chronicled, both by Tracy and by Pat O'Brien, with whom he soon met up again, because, coincidentally, O'Brien, too, had tried out for the American Academy of Dramatic Arts and had been accepted.

To condense the chronicle, both Tracy and O'Brien had to live on the thirty dollars a month veterans' benefit they received from the government. At first, Tracy took a miserable furnished room on West 56th Street, but then he and O'Brien pooled resources and rented a slightly larger room ("twelve-by-twelve, with two iron bedsteads taking up nearly all the space") on West 96th Street. They both later wrote about these Dickensian lodgings, but their memories were inconsistent. O'Brien, for example, recalled "our kindly Irish landlady, Mrs. Brown," whereas Tracy referred to "our kindly Irish landlady, Mrs. Cornelius Muldowney." Both, however, agreed on the fact that the beneath-the-roof room "was as cold as the Arctic in winter and as hot as the Egyptian desert in summer," and that they mainly subsisted "on a diet of pretzels, rice and water" as their government money ran out towards the end of every month.

Tracy wrote, "I was too proud to write home for more money because I knew my father probably had a good idea of what was happening and thought it would be the best way to cure me of my crazy ambition." On the other hand, he added, "There's something about going hungry that makes you discover the utmost of your resources. For an actor, it's a swell experience, because it gives you insight in characterizations you couldn't play otherwise. I don't know anything that gives you more sympathy and understanding of others in similar circumstances than an empty stomach."

Both Tracy and O'Brien did well in their drama classes at the Academy, where the school's director, Charles Jehlinger, remembered Tracy, years later, as "a responsive student with a good voice you'd be able to hear at the top of the second balcony, but who was easily bored with the exercises of movement that all actors should learn. He was happiest when we did plays." Concerning O'Brien, Jehlinger said, "He had much talent, but was impatient and undisciplined." O'Brien did not finish the one-year course at the Academy, and, because he no longer was a student, his veterans' benefit ran out. Tracy saved them from total starvation by getting them non-speaking parts as robots in Karel Capek's now-classic science fiction play *R.U.R.*, which was being produced by the Theater Guild. They each earned fifteen dollars a week, twenty-five dollars for Tracy when he was promoted to a speaking part (one line). The play kept them in pretzels up until the time Tracy graduated from the Academy, in March 1923.

Then they were in *real* trouble, because now Tracy's veterans' benefit ran out, too. *R.U.R.* had closed and Tracy, who had appeared in three of the Academy's graduation plays, had received no offers from the producers who attended the event, whereas other students had. The "pretty boys" were still in demand, and, as Tracy learned, there was a lingering prejudice against Irish actors on Broadway, perhaps because there were too many of them all trying to make it at the same time. Ethnic bigotry of all kinds was still pretty flagrant in 1923, and even practised by producers of the same ethnic stock.

It was a tough time for Tracy and O'Brien. To keep laundry costs down, they wore one another's clothing; they habitually fell behind in their rent, and only evaded eviction because of the kindness of Mrs. Brown/Muldowney who, as a counterpoint to the producers, had vast sympathy for destitute young actors of her own, Irish, extraction. O'Brien got an occasional bit part in a stock company production in nearby New Jersey or Westchester County; Tracy kept making the rounds of the Broadway casting offices and took odd jobs, like selling magazine subscriptions. O'Brien was finally hired by a theatre group in Plainfield, New Jersey, and left, wearing a pair of white flannel trousers furnished by Tracy.

It was June 1923. Alone now, Tracy's feelings of desperation became acute. He later wrote that he had lost all confidence in himself, and was ready to give up and go home to Milwaukee. He would do anything his father wanted; go into the trucking business, enter a seminary, anything. In fact, as he continued to make the casting rounds, he more and more found himself dropping into Catholic churches, for prayer and solace, something he had not done since his Marquette Academy days.

This combination of persistence and prayer apparently paid off. He came home one day to find his landlady waiting for him with a telegram that had arrived while he was out. One of the casting people had recommended him to Leonard Wood Jr who was forming a new stock company in White Plains, New York, and needed a versatile actor to play many roles, ranging from comedy to melodrama. Tracy could scarcely believe his eyes. He resisted the temptation to go out and get drunk, and sent a collect wire to Wood. A return telegram came back from Wood, enclosing a money order for his first week's salary of forty dollars. Tracy paid off Mrs. Brown/Muldowney. *Then* he went out and got drunk.

Chapter Six

As the result of this exchange of telegrams, Tracy ended up with more than a job. As he boarded the train to White Plains, in Grand Central Station, he noticed a striking-looking young woman in an elegant green dress. She had fashionably coiffed dark hair which set off the alabaster quality of her fair skin. She had with her an inordinate amount of baggage for the short trip to any possible destination in Westchester County.

Tracy wondered about her from time to time, as he sat in the dusty coach, pondering his future. When he got off the train in White Plains, just thirty-odd minutes later, there was the young woman in the green dress, descending to the platform with all her luggage. As Tracy described it later, he immediately deduced that she was an actress headed for the same Leonard Wood stock company for which he was going to work. He engaged her in conversation and discovered that his assumption was correct. She said her name was

Louise Treadwell, and that Wood had hired her to be the leading lady in the plays he was planning to produce. As they shared a cab to the theatre, they engaged in the usual actor chitchat; "Where have you worked?" etc. Tracy was enthralled to learn that Miss Treadwell had toured as the lead in a well-known play, *Nothing But the Truth,* and had made it to Broadway in a secondary role in *The Pigeon,* which he had seen from a 75-cent seat in the second balcony. "I fell in love on the spot," Tracy recalled.

His instant infatuation with Louise was a new experience for him. He had only sparingly dated girls before this, and, as Sterling Holloway, a classmate at the Academy of Dramatic Arts, said, "I remember that he was very shy with women. Also, he was broke most of the time and didn't have the money to go out much. When he came up with a few spare bucks, he'd usually go out and get swoggled with Pat O'Brien."

So love blossomed quickly for Tracy in the promising theatre environment of the stock company in White Plains. And Louise seems to have been equally swiftly attracted to him, too. She, like him, had led a lonely, sometimes troubled life. Born into a highly respectable Episcopalian family in New Castle, Pennsylvania, she was very close to her mother, Alliene, who gave her singing and dancing lessons, and even accompanied her when she got occasional work in vaudeville on the stage in New York and Chicago. At times, in fact, the mother-pressure became too much for her, and Louise took time out to go to Lake Erie College, where she graduated with honours in 1917, but, at the urgings of Alliene, returned to the stage in a chorus-line role. She was rebellious, frequently fleeing back to New Castle, but, when her mother died suddenly in 1919, "the guilt caught up with me", as she put it. She tried working for a while as a teacher and on the local newspaper in New Castle. Soon, however, she went back to the stage, as her mother had wished. That's when she got her roles in *Nothing But the Truth* and *The Pigeon*.

It is not generally known, but Louise was four years older than Tracy. Compared with his own scant experience in the theatre, he thought of her as a star, but, as she said, *"I* knew I wasn't." In White Plains, she was the leading lady, and Tracy only played bit parts, but, she said,

"I loved him because he was so earnest, so attentive, and such a good actor. With a single line, boomed out in that strong voice of his, he could instantly command the attention of the audience. Leonard Wood's company in White Plains went out of business in a few months, but, when I was offered a job with the Repertory Theater of Cincinnati, I told Stuart Walker, who owned the stock company, that I wanted Spencer Tracy as my leading man. Stuart grumbled, but finally agreed. By then, I also knew that I wanted Spencer Tracy as my husband."

Tracy proposed to Louise a few weeks after they arrived in Cincinnati. They were playing opposite each other, at the time, in a play called *Buddies,* in which, to Stuart Walker's surprise, "the previously untested kid amazed me with his ability to memorize the entire script overnight, and with his instinctive power to grab and hold an audience." It was not too amazing to Walker, who later became a movie producer at Paramount Pictures, when he learned that Tracy had proposed marriage to Louise, and that she had accepted. "I knew it was in the cards," he said, "by the way they looked at each other when they first showed up in Cincinnati."

Tracy later said that he did *not* know it was in the cards until the moment it happened. He wrote that he did not feel worthy of Louise: "She was a great lady, a well-organized lady, all the things I wasn't, so what would she want with me? You could have knocked me over with a feather when she said yes, right off the bat. We talked about her being a Protestant and me being a Catholic, but I said that's the way it was with Mom and Dad. In fact, Louise reminded me of my mother, a lot."

They were married on 12 September 1923, probably by a court clerk, since the record does not specify that any clergyman was involved. There was no time for a honeymoon. They had to finish their run in *Buddies*.

Then the honeymoon was delayed again, because Tracy got his first offer to join the cast of a play that was headed for Broadway. It was *A Royal Fandango,* starring the great Ethel Barrymore. Tracy was to play a secondary role, a detective. Another detective was a newcomer like Tracy, named Edward G. Robinson.

The Tracys rented a small apartment in Brooklyn for the run of the play, which was not very long. *A Royal Fandango* bombed with the critics and closed in a few weeks. An unsigned review in the old *New York World* mentioned Tracy and Robinson: "They looked as though they had been picked up by the property man." Without Tracy's $100 a week salary, the newlyweds were in tough financial shape. Worse, Louise told Tracy she was pregnant, and did not want to risk going to work on the road in winter stock where she had some offers.

Tracy did not even have time to savour the news of his impending fatherhood. He feverishly made the rounds of the booking offices again, but there was nothing for him in New York. Finally, in desperation, he called his parents in Milwaukee. His father once again insisted that Spencer "give up this foolishness and come back and work with me in the trucking business." (Since Spencer's marriage, John Tracy no longer mentioned the priesthood.) Tracy's mother, Carrie, was much more compassionate. She had met Louise and liked her enormously (she later expounded on the similarities between herself and Louise in a *Milwaukee Journal* interview). Carrie suggested that Louise come to live with them in Milwaukee until the baby was born, freeing Spencer to go "on the road," to continue to make his living that way as an actor, if he so desired. Louise and Spencer gratefully accepted.

"The road," in the early 1920s, was the life-blood of all dramatic arts in the United States. Movie theatres had not yet cemented their universal grip on the country, and people were still entranced by the prospect of seeing live actors, no matter how insipid or moth-eaten the plays. Every city and good-sized town had a permanent stock-company theatre, with permanent and itinerant actors. The trend blossomed as it never had before, for a few years, at least, until talking pictures came along after Al Jolson's *The Jazz Singer* in 1927. Until then, the road was the spawning ground, the basic training programme for nearly all American actors, even the great ones destined for Broadway and Hollywood—actors like Fredric March, Cary Grant, Jeanette MacDonald, and many, many more. The road was also the spawning ground for great playwrights and directors, such as Sidney Howard and John Cromwell.

But the road was a rugged life. Pat O'Brien

wrote, "You'd latch on with a stock company, and it would be a new play starting every Sunday. You were constantly acting in one play, while rehearsing next week's play and learning the script of the third week's play. It was a never-ending cycle of hard work."

For Tracy, with his phenomenal memory, this aspect of the road did not faze him much. Rather, he complained about the physical and financial hardships: "The trains were as bumpy as a frog's back; the hotels were boot-camps for roaches and bugs. I'd make about seventy-five dollars a week, and by the time I went out for a couple of steaks and some drinks, and sent a few bucks home, I'd be broke again."

On 26 June 1924, Louise gave birth to a son. Tracy quit his short-term job with a Pittsburgh stock company and left the road for a few weeks, to be with her in Milwaukee. The infant boy seemed strong and healthy in all respects, and they named him John, after Spencer's father. Now, it was all the more difficult for Tracy to return to the road, but, as he lamented, "It was the only way I knew how to make money for my little family."

So back he went, this time to W. H. Wright's company in Grand Rapids, Michigan. At least it was close enough for him to make a quick trip home on his one day off. By now, Tracy had developed a good reputation as a steady player with good power, and it was much easier for him to get work. W. H. Wright, for example, had used him in his Pittsburgh company, then wanted him for Grand Rapids, and later for Lima, Ohio. Tracy played drama, light comedy, even musicals — although he was almost totally tone-deaf, he danced passably well. In Grand Rapids, he played lead roles opposite the fine actress Selena Royle, who commented, "Spencer was a strange man of many gloomy moods, but when he walked on a stage before an audience, he seemed to forget what was troubling him. He was completely natural, and it was a pleasure to work with him."

(Strangely, I got a reasonably similar paraphrase of this quotation from nearly every actress he ever appeared with, on the screen as well as on stage.)

While Tracy was working with Miss Royle in Grand Rapids, Louise Tracy made a tragic discovery about her son. This is how she detailed the moment when it happened:

"John was ten months old. He was taking a nap. I thought I should waken him. I slammed the screen door as I went into the room where he was asleep in his crib. He didn't waken. Then I called to him. He didn't waken. I always had touched him before, and I did it now, ever so gently. His eyes flew open, and he was looking at me, and I knew he was deaf."

A doctor confirmed her worst fears. An accompanying fear was her dread of telling Tracy, whose growing moodiness and cantankerousness on his visits home had become a source of irritation between them. She delayed saying anything about John's disability until, inevitably, Tracy found out himself, about three weeks later.

It was a Sunday afternoon in Brooklyn, where Tracy had gone for a season of winter stock in the Montauk Theater. Towards the end of the run, he had become terribly lonely, and asked Louise to come with the baby and join him for a while. As the story has been recounted by both Tracy and Louise, he was playing with the little boy, and, when the infant's back was turned, Tracy shouted and clapped his hands, but John did not respond. "What's the matter with this kid?" Tracy asked his wife. "He doesn't seem to hear me."

"No," said Louise. "He doesn't hear you—and he never will."

"What do you mean?" he said.

"He was born totally deaf," replied Mrs Tracy. "I've known about it for three weeks, but I couldn't bring myself to tell you."

Pat O'Brien told me, "What happened next was typical of both Louise and Spence. Louise suffered, and took her boy to doctors to find out what could be done. Spence suffered, and went out and got drunk. It was the first *big* drunk of his life, as far as I know. He was gone for days and finally was found holed up in the St George Hotel there in Brooklyn."

Said Lynne Overman, another actor from Milwaukee, who had become Tracy's close friend on the road, "My feeling is that some good and some bad came out of this business of John's deafness. On the good side, Spence actually was a very lazy man, but the need for giving John all the help possible to overcome his handicap made Spence work so hard at his craft that he became one of the finest actors in the world.

"On the bad side: it increased Spence's natural tendencies to escape from his problems, in the worst kinds of ways."

Again, the Spencer Tracy paradox.

Chapter Seven

From 1925 to 1929, Tracy immersed himself in his work, with a fervour he had never exhibited before. He suffered the hardships of being on the road, but made no further complaints. After his discovery of John's deafness, he went back to the W. H. Wright company in the Powers Theater in Grand Rapids. He fought with Wright because of what Wright called "Tracy's sullenness and uncooperative attitude with the press," and got fired. (In the years to come, however, Wright kept taking Tracy back "because skilled actors of his calibre are rare, and you have to put up with their foibles.")

From Grand Rapids, Tracy went to the Trent Theater Stock Company in Trenton, New Jersey, where, for the first time, his drinking interfered with his work. He reeled on stage for a performance of *The Song and Dance Man,* and barely got through the evening, mostly because the play, written by George M. Cohan for himself, was loosely constructed to accommodate Cohan's ad libs. Tracy threw the other actors off stride, however, and he was fired. He was saved only by the fact that he was the company's leading man, and at the time, in the middle of the winter season, no one else was available.

He had drawn much closer to Louise because of their joint concern for John, but Trenton was "a period of major depression for Spencer," according to his co-star, Ethel Remey. Back at home, Tracy flew into unexpected rages, and sulked because he felt that despite working so hard, his career seemed to be going nowhere. He later wrote, "I had done more than fifty plays, and a lot of guys, without my talent, were making it on Broadway, while I was still stuck in the sticks."

But finally that was changed when Selena Royle, his leading lady from Grand Rapids, recommended Tracy to George M. Cohan for a new play, *Yellow*, which the great actor-impresario was about to produce on Broadway. Miss Royle had already been chosen for the cast, and had considerable influence because she was the daughter of Edwin Milton Royle, a playwright whom Cohan greatly admired. In any event, Tracy was hired for the secondary role of Jimmy Wilkes, a bank clerk, receiving eighth billing behind Miss Royle, Chester Morris and others. The play was to be a major turning point for him.

Cohan was very much like Tracy, cantankerous, sometimes mean, always irreverent. That's why everyone was shocked, when in a rehearsal at the National Theater, he suddenly stopped bellowing at the other actors and stared at Tracy. According to Damon Runyon, who was present at the rehearsal, and wrote about the incident, "In front of the entire company, Cohan said, 'Spencer Tracy, you're the best damn actor I ever saw,' and walked out of the theater."

Yellow was not a very good play (it was a slight piece about a young man who gets his girlfriend pregnant), but the Cohan name gave it a successful run of more than four months on Broadway. The critics, however, barely took notice of Tracy in his secondary role, despite Cohan's pre-opening extravagant praise of him. In later years, Tracy, in turn, gave similar extravagant praise to Cohan, saying, "The old master taught me everything I know about underplaying and timing," which, said Pat O'Brien, "was bullshit, because Spence had instinctively learned *everything* about acting before he got to do *Yellow.*"

There is no doubt, however, that Cohan became Tracy's principal mentor. He used him in two subsequent plays, one of which, *The Baby Cyclone,* he told him during the run of *Yellow,* he was going to write "specifically for you."

By now, Tracy was officially "a Broadway actor," and he was invited to join the prestigious Lambs Club on West 44th Street in New York. He did a lot of nocturnal carousing there with Lynne Overman, Frank McHugh and Pat O'Brien. Another of the carousers was Chester Morris, who said, "The rest of us drank for fun; Spence drank like he was trying to forget something, probably the deafness of his kid, and lots of nights we had to haul him back home to Louise."

As for Louise, she was growing more and more restive about Tracy's late nights in the Great White Way. She kept telling him she wanted to return to acting, with him as her leading man; a recreation of the happy days they had had together when they first met in White Plains. Tracy, who had made thousands of dollars, more than he ever had in his whole life, during the run of Cohan's *Yellow,* wanted instead to wait for the new play Cohan had promised to write for him. But, possibly out of guilt for the hard time he had given Louise since her revelation of John's deafness, he agreed to work with her again. But it would have to be on the road, in stock. He knew that there was no chance that any producer would want to team them on Broadway.

To satisfy Louise, Tracy called his old fall-back employer, W. H. Wright, and learned that the producer was opening a new stock company at the Faurot Opera House in Lima, Ohio. Wright readily agreed to take Louise and Tracy as his leading lady and man in Lima. He was able to advertise that "Tracy is fresh from his appearance in *Yellow,* on Broadway, and Miss Treadwell has had unlimited experience in the musical comedy field."

Lima was a disaster for both Tracy and Louise. The town had previously been just a one-night stand way-stop for road shows moving on to Chicago from Pittsburgh. Tracy found this a comedown and brooded at being back in the sticks after his mini-triumph on Broadway. Louise was ill part of the time and found it difficult to take care of John while readjusting to the backbreaking new-play-every-week schedule. They had signed on for four months, but, after nine weeks of plays like *Laff That Off* and *Applesauce,* both were happy to get out when Tracy received a wire from George M. Cohan, notifying him that he was ready to go into production on Broadway with *The Baby Cyclone.* The Tracys resigned from the Wright Players on 26 June 1927, and fled back to New York. It was the last time Louise ever set foot on a stage as an actress.

For Tracy, "The return to Broadway got all the juices flowing in me again." It was a wild and exciting place, in which he was now prepared to settle for good. Prohibition was in full swing. Everyone in Tracy's income bracket had a personal bootlegger and dozens of speakeasies abutted the theatre district. It was the heyday of later to become respectable, but then illegal, drinking and eating establishments like the 21 Club. In the speakeasies, notorious gangsters—Legs Diamond, Waxey Gordon, Bugsy Siegel—rubbed shoulders with the elite of the Broadway stage. Tracy said he was in a speakeasy called LaHiff's, when he was bought a drink by a man who openly identified himself as Albert Anastasia. "He talked to me," recalled Tracy, "about the bootlegger connections at the Lambs Club. I didn't know much about that, so he switched the subject to George M. Cohan's plays and how he could muscle in on them as an angel. I didn't know much about that, either. The guy left, and the next day I read that he had been bumped off in a barber chair at the Park Central Hotel while he was getting a facial." (As he frequently did, Tracy was confusing his time-frames. Anastasia was not killed until the 1950's, when Tracy undoubtedly had met him again.)

Along with the speakeasies, a host of high-class brothels existed on the side streets off the Great White Way. Toots Shor, later a noted restaurateur, and a good friend of Tracy's, was then a bouncer at LaHiff's. Shor told me,

"Spence was a shy guy. He started out by asking me who were the hookers hanging out in LaHiff's joint. He'd approach them but couldn't get anywhere because he always got eased out by some flashier guy. Then he asked me about whorehouses in the neighborhood. I sent him to a place called Lu's. Lu was a good friend of mine and she told me Spence became a pretty good customer until one night, when he was loaded and beat up one of her girls and busted up the joint. I then sent him to Sally's. I never heard any complaints about him from Sally. She said he liked to have his joint copped but who doesn't?"

Since Tracy was then in long rehearsals for *The Baby Cyclone,* and away from their apartment off West End Avenue for many hours every day and night, Louise Tracy seems to have been unaware of these side excursions. Mostly, she was concerned about Tracy's close association with George M. Cohan, as lucrative as it had become. Cohan by now considered Tracy one of his prize protégés. Though only twenty-two years older, he had formed a father-son relationship with the promising young actor. Cohan wrote,

"Tracy reminded me of myself as a young man. He was brash and always stood up to me and took my guff. We needled each other back and forth all the time, and instead of getting mad, I'd break up when he told me to go f—myself. He didn't have much of a singing voice, but I figured he could fake his way through revivals of some of my best musical comedies. Until the time he went into the movies, I was planning to use him in my role in a new version of my greatest hit, *The Song and Dance Man.*"

But at forty-nine, Cohan was an embittered man. He had fought an acrimonious campaign against the founding of the actors' union, Equity, and was continuing to work only because Equity gave him a special waiver not compelling him to join. As a result, there was much resentment against him on Broadway, and his work was suffering. Although his name-value still attracted audiences, his shows were called old-fashioned and inconsequential by the critics. This is what bothered Louise Tracy most. She wrote that, "Spencer, at that stage of his career, should be doing more important work, no matter how much he had learned from Mr Cohan."

Cohan's *The Baby Cyclone* opened at the Henry Miller Theater on 12 September 1927. It was another piece of fluff, this time a farce about two couples incessantly arguing over a pet dog. The play did nothing to enhance Tracy's reputation, but it ran for 184 days. He was back on Broadway to stay. As soon as *The Baby Cyclone* ended its run, Cohan put Tracy into another one of his plays, *Whispering Friends,* as a replacement for the male lead, William Harrigan.

By now, however, Tracy was beset by still another pending tragedy. His 51-year-old father, after a series of reverses in his business career, back in Milwaukee, had gone to work for General Motors. He was then transferred to New York. Tracy was happy to be so close, geographically, to his parents again, who rented a small apartment a few blocks from where Spence and Louise lived on West 73rd Street. Carrie became an invaluable help to Louise and little John, now four years old and still speechless because of his hearing handicap.

One day Carrie broke the news to Tracy that his father had cancer. Tracy was devastated. He later told me, "In my love-hate relationship with Dad, no matter how much we disagreed, I always had looked to him as a tower of strength where I always could retreat. Now, could the tower be crumbling?"

Tracy did everything he could to atone for his past differences with his father. He visited him as much as he could, both at home and later when his dad was hospitalized. The senior Tracys had come to see him three times in *The Baby Cyclone,* and his father told him, "You're doing very well, son, at what you've chosen to be your life's work."

One night, George M. Cohan came backstage at *Whispering Friends,* and had the sad task of informing Tracy that his father had died.

Another image of Tracy from the later years:

It is 1954, and I am on the set of There's No Business Like Show Business, *to interview Ethel Merman. The interview falls through and I chat with Frank McHugh over coffee in the 20th Century-Fox commissary. The subject of his good friend, Spencer Tracy, comes up.*

After much reminiscence about the old days in New York, McHugh says,

"You know, I'll never forget the time Spence rolled into the Lambs Club maybe three or four weeks after his father died. He was half in the bag, but not blotto, like he sometimes got. He said, 'My father always wanted me to be a priest, but I disappointed him. Then, at the end, he said he was proud that I was a good actor, but he never lived long enough to see me in anything decent.'

"What I can't forget is what Spence said next, after he cried a little bit. He said, 'Maybe I got the guilt. Maybe that's why I do my best when I play priests in my pictures, like Father Mullin in San Francisco and Father Flanagan in Boys Town.' Old Spence, he knocked me right on my Irish-Catholic ass when he said that."

Chapter Eight

Insomnia was a problem that had afflicted Tracy for many years, and which would continue to dog him until the end of his life. It became particularly acute for him in times of great stress. The period after the death of his father was one of those times. He said, "I tried sleeping pills, and even knockout drops, but nothing helped." (He was referring to barbiturates and chloral hydrate, both of which he took regularly all his life, and which, in combination with alcohol, caused some of his most traumatic, and sometimes near-fatal, drunken binges.)

Tracy said the insomnia began when he was in the Navy where he spent a good deal of time worrying about having disappointed his father. Later, when he became an actor, he developed chronic sleeplessness, he said, because of the enormous effort he put into quickly memorizing scripts "which then boiled around in my dreams and kept waking me up, because the lines in the dreams were all wrong and I had to fix them." Tracy's pattern was to go to sleep early with his pills, which would only work for three or four hours, then get up and stay up through the rest of the night and the early morning. Fortunately, he didn't repeat the dosage of sleeping pills upon awakening because, as he frequently revealed to friends, he had a real fear of dying and he knew too many people who had overdosed on barbiturates. He was less careful with alcohol, but it probably was the same reasoning which made him a periodic, rather than a constant alcoholic, with periods of reflective sobriety in between.

The acute insomnia which he suffered after his father's death, and the accompanying self-flagellation, apparently caused the lines to deepen in his face. Noting this at the Lambs Club, Chester Morris said (not with any humorous intent), "Spence is getting to be the only guy I know under fifty you could describe as 'craggy looking.'" Morris had previously commented on a deepening of the facial lines when Tracy had learned about the deafness of his son.

Being craggy-looking at twenty-nine was a problem for Tracy. The theatre of the 1920s was still the heyday of the matinee idol, the perfect-featured male lead who attracted the ladies to the matinee performances in droves. All the fears about "pretty boys" (once expressed to Tracy by old Franklin Havens Sargent at the American Academy of Dramatic Arts) had come to pass. Now, in 1929, Tracy did not know what to do about it, but wise, practical-minded Louise Tracy *did*.

Louise said that she told Tracy,

"Forget George M. Cohan and all that fluff he's writing now. Forget the light comedy, which is practically all you've been doing since I've known you. You can't compete with those tall, handsome F. Scott Fitzgerald-type guys. Do you want to keep playing the wronged husband or the buffoon? No. Your ace in the hole is that you're a terrific actor who can play heavy drama, which the pretty boys can't. That's the kind of play you should be looking for."

Tracy listened. But then, as later, he was a very poor judge of scripts, and it took him a while to get on the right track. He did four plays in 1929, all of them flops. One of them, *Dread,* closed out of town before it reached Broadway. *Nigger Rich* and *Veneer* each opened and closed in less than a month in New York. Only Warren Lawrence's play, *Conflict,* came close to what Louise was talking about, and it, too, lasted only thirty-seven days in the Fulton Theater on Broadway. In *Conflict,* Tracy played a wimp of a clerk who became a flying ace in World War I, and was then destroyed by his inability to handle his fame when he returned to civilian life. His performance was mentioned by *Theater Magazine's* critic as "One of the most notable of the season." It also caught the attention of a group of young entrepreneurs, newcomers to the New York stage, who were preparing an exceedingly heavy drama for the 1930 season, and who had previously thought of Tracy only as a skilled light-comedy actor.

The newcomers were producer Herman Shumlin, then only twenty-seven; director Chester Erskine, twenty-three, and playwright John Wexley, an obscure ex-actor, also twenty-three. At the time, Wexley's play was called "All the World Wonders." He had based it on the true story of a convict named Robert Blake who had set down his thoughts as he awaited execution in Death Row. Wexley changed the name of his protagonist to Killer Mears (to be played by Tracy), and, after the Auburn Prison riot erupted in upstate New York in January 1930, he added a prison break and riot to Act Two of his play. He also changed the name of the play to *The Last Mile,* now a common expression in the English language for doomed convicts on their way to the electric chair or the gas chamber.

With all the light-hearted junk that dominated the American stage in that era, the script gave promise of becoming one of Broadway's first attempts at *théâtre vérité*. Tracy read the play but was not too happy with it. George M. Cohan advised him against doing it, "because the people want to continue to see light comedy in their entertainment." (It was just after the stock market crash and the beginning of the Great Depression.) Impresario Sam Harris, however, saw its potential and booked it into his theatre. Louise Tracy also saw its potential. So, reluctantly, Tracy signed to play Killer Mears.

Tracy was about to turn thirty and wrote that he felt uncomfortable with the younger Shumlin, Erskine and Wexley. In turn, Erskine and Wexley retained their doubts about Tracy, mainly because of all the fluff he had previously performed in. Only producer Herman Shumlin, who was to move on to genuine greatness in the theatre, believed in Tracy's innate ability to handle the role.

The tryout of *The Last Mile,* in Hartford, Connecticut, did not go well. Tracy was sure the play was going to bomb and brooded at the Lambs Club as he awaited the Broadway opening on 13 February 1930.

Pat O'Brien, too, had doubts about his friend's play. He wrote:

"It had an all-male cast, which to me seemed a little dangerous at the time. I recall Broadway had had few if any productions without the girls. Tracy returned glum and sagging from the break-in at Hartford.

" 'Boys, I'm in one helluva flop. I'd like to pull out, but I have a run of the play contract.'

"He pleaded with us, 'Don't see the show — I've got no confidence in it.' Spence had been honest when he told us he was in a flop. The try out audience had been anything but responsive. 'Their receptivity was as cold as the Yukon.' Spence thought he was in a bomb.

"But I bought a gallery ticket on opening night and witnessed a one-man performance of amazing power, of near-greatness — Spence as the condemned man. At the final curtain, the audience stood and cheered. It was a spine-tingling production, the first of the powerful prison yarns. All the actors were fine, but Spence was an overnight sensation."

O'Brien was not the only enthusiast. The tough New York critics agreed, without exception, that the relentlessly realistic drama had set a milestone on Broadway and that Tracy's performance was brilliant. The *New York Times'* Brooks Atkinson, never previously a particular admirer of Tracy's, wrote that the play was, "A taut, searing drama with a motive" and that "Mears is a killer acted with muscular determination by Spencer Tracy and acted well."

So, in his thirtieth year, Tracy had finally made it big, and in a way which would have pleased his father. After ten years of travail, he was in a smash hit, as a result of which *he* was about to become a cucumber thrown into the Hollywood pickle barrel.

Chapter Nine

With the first talking picture, Al Jolson's *The Jazz Singer* in 1927, the movie industry had begun an unprecedented all-out raid on Broadway. Many of the silent-film stars could not speak too well, or, as in the case of John Gilbert, spoke in a funny way. So the New York theatre became the principal hunting ground for the Hollywood talent scouts. They quickly found Fredric March, Bette Davis and others, but Tracy was generally overlooked. He had screen-tested for Fox, MGM and Universal in New York, and had made four Vitaphone short-subjects for Warner Brothers (each requiring just one day's filming), but all had been fruitless and disastrous experiences for him. He had been told, "You're too ugly to be a leading man, and not ugly enough to be a villain." So he had decided to forget Hollywood and to devote himself to his art, on the stage.

But then, three weeks into the run of *The Last Mile,* the old Fox Film Corporation dispatched director John Ford to New York to see several plays. His objective was to find two good actors for a still-unwritten film about the Auburn, New York, prison riot, to be called *Up the River*. Ford recalled that Fox gave him tickets for five plays on five different nights, but that he saw *The Last Mile* on the first night, and went back to see it again on each of the remaining four nights. He was enchanted with Tracy's performance. Ford, a hard-drinking Irishman (who had been directing pictures since he was twenty-two and had just finished a fine film, *Men Without Women)* also became enchanted with Tracy's Hibernian carousing in an all-night roister at the Lambs Club.

Ford took Tracy to Fox's New York headquarters and Tracy was signed to a one-picture deal, over the protests of the casting executives who remembered Tracy's Fox screen test, in which he had been made up as a bearded sailor who conversed in grunts. "Never mind," said Ford, "I want him." Almost as an afterthought, he also told them to sign another actor for the second role he had to fill for *Up the River*. He had seen *this* actor in the only matinee performance he had gone to that week. It was Humphrey Bogart.

Louise exulted. She didn't think Tracy "photographed well," but she sensed that a good director like Ford could make his strong personality come through on the screen. She also liked the idea of the salary he would earn, eight hundred dollars a week.

Tracy wheedled six weeks' leave of absence from *The Last Mile* producer, Herman Shumlin, and came west alone, leaving Louise and John behind. Already nervous at this excursion into unknown territory, he suffered an anxiety attack when he picked up a newspaper on the long train trip, and read a rave review about a new MGM prison picture, *The Big House,* starring Robert Montgomery, Wallace Beery and his old friend, Chester Morris.

When he arrived in Los Angeles, John Ford came to see Tracy in his hotel room and airily told him, "Don't worry. Because of *The Big House,* we're going to make *our* prison picture into a comedy." It was not so easily done, and Winfield Sheehan, the head of the studio, seriously considered scrapping the film, along with Tracy and Bogart. But it finally came off. *Up the River* turned out to be a rather silly exercise about a woman convict, played by Claire Luce, an attempt to fleece a small town, and the thwarting of the scheme through a prison escape by Tracy and Warren Hymer.

Bogart's role was a relatively minor one, but it was the beginning of what was to become a lifelong friendship between him and Tracy. When the Fox executives saw the electricity generated by Tracy in his scenes with Bogart, they offered Tracy an immediate long-term contract, effective on signing. Tracy refused, saying he was an honourable man and had to go back to New York to finish the Broadway run of *The Last Mile*. Fox offered him more money. Again he refused and returned to New York.

In November 1930, the play finished its run and Tracy finally signed with Fox, at even more money than they had previously offered, $1,200 a week. Tracy, Louise and John moved to Hollywood shortly after Thanksgiving that year. Fox put them up in a bungalow at a sprawling gaudy hotel called The Garden of Allah. (They later moved into a rented house on Franklin Avenue in Hollywood.)

The Great Depression had begun shortly before Tracy had opened in *The Last Mile,* and Tracy had nervously noted its effects in New York; bread lines, plummeting theatre attendance, suicides, unemployed actors selling apples on Broadway street corners. Little of this was in evidence when he settled in at The Garden of Allah. With the film industry's inflated salaries (the first big wage cuts were not to come until 1933), Hollywood had the aspects of a Wild West boom town. At Hollywood parties, fresh flowers were floated in swimming pools and multicoloured bubbles emanated from special bubble-making machines. Fight nights at the Hollywood Legion Stadium were jammed with movie people. The streets were festooned with expensive Maserati and Cord motor cars.

The city, in its transformation from a sleepy

collection of rural villages into the film capital of the world, was still unformed. Much of the San Fernando Valley was rural, with vast expanses of bean fields and orange groves. There were yet-unpaved streets in what are now Beverly Hills and Brentwood, but there was a bridle path for rich and famous equestrians, running through the middle of Sunset Boulevard and turning down the now-famous shopping street, Rodeo Drive.

The "old money" (from oil and land wealth) lived to the east, in areas like Hancock Park, and discriminated against the new movie-industry wealth (there were many Jews, Irish and "other foreigners"), pushing the film people further and further to the west, and opening up new clusters of affluent settlement in the Beverly Hills canyons, Brentwood, Pacific Palisades and the Santa Monica beaches, where Marion Davies' ninety-room mansion, on the so-called Gold Coast, had grass strips laid over the sand.

In Hollywood itself, the fleshpots thrived, causing temptation of varied kinds for Tracy. Bootleg booze, illegal gambling casinos, loose young women aspiring to become actresses, could be found everywhere. A short distance away, the soon to be famous Sunset Strip was built up on the north side of the street, with glamorous night clubs like Mocambo and Ciro's. The south side of the street was undeveloped, with only an occasional establishment overlooking the mostly open spaces of what is now the city of West Hollywood.

In the 8400 block of the south side of Sunset Boulevard were the Clover Club, a gambling house, and Lee Francis', a whorehouse used by the studios to provide female companionship for visiting foreign movie distributors (on one famous occasion, all the girls were dyed blonde, top and bottom, to satisfy the desire of a group of South Americans). It was here that Tracy had his first brush with the law in Southern California. He was arrested while erratically attempting to back a borrowed car out of the driveway of 8428 Sunset Boulevard, between Lee Francis' and the Clover Club. The police records state that "Tracy resisted the Sheriff's deputies and had to be restrained with handcuffs and leg straps". He was booked as a drunk in County Jail, from which he was soon sprung at the intervention of his studio, Fox.

It was another troubled period for Tracy. His son, John, now was six years old, and, in addition to his deafness, had also suffered an attack of polio. He had fortunately recovered from the polio with only mild muscle damage. Mrs. Tracy was now devoting herself almost entirely to the boy. Four years earlier, she had taken him to the famous Dr. Harvey Cushing in Boston. Louise told me, "Dr. Cushing said, 'There's nothing I can do, Mrs. Tracy, but I just want you to know that you're blessed among women. In helping John, you can lead a wonderfully interesting life.' "

Louise had taken Dr. Cushing's advice seriously and literally. She had immersed herself in special courses to learn how to teach the deaf to read lips, and, eventually, to speak. She worked incessantly with the boy, "perhaps," said Pat O'Brien, "to the exclusion of Spence."

Tracy told me, "I tried to help with John's lip reading, but I was no damn good at it. I'd come home after working all day and I'd lose patience. Louise might have spent hours trying to get John to understand and say a word like 'shoe' without showing it to him. I'd just pick up the damned shoe and spoil everything she had been trying to do. So, eventually I backed off, and left it all to her. I loved the boy and it was painful and frustrating not to be able to help. I concentrated more and more on my work."

But his work was frustrating, too. In those days, it was not unusual for a movie star to make as many as eight pictures a year, and Tracy filled his quota. He became increasingly dissatisfied, however, with the quality of the films to which he was assigned by Fox. Among them were such unmemorable potboilers as *She Wanted a Millionaire*, *Sky Devils*, *Young America* and *Society Girl*. He worked with such leading ladies as Jean Harlow, Joan Bennett and Bette Davis, who, except for

Miss Davis, a dedicated rebel herself, were more sanguine about the sleaziness of the Fox product in those days.

Miss Harlow, then twenty, was a neophyte like Tracy, but with no stage background. She was, however, a finishing-school graduate and smarter than she seemed. Her first encounters with Tracy, on a film called *Goldie* (originally titled "A Girl in Every Port") were not pleasant ones. She said, "He was a guy who came out of New York and believed that his movie contract gave him a license to feel." According to Harlow, Tracy used his hands on every female in sight, from the script girl to her. She said, "We still were in the old Fox studio on Western Avenue in Hollywood, and the walls of the dressing rooms were very thin. Spence would coax some star-struck girl inside, and then we could hear the squeaking of the springs in his couch."

But Harlow eventually became fond of Tracy when he took an interest in helping her as an actress. She said, "He told me, 'Goddamit, stop putting on airs and just talk like you naturally do. For God's sake, stop trying to sound like the Queen of England.' " She followed his advice, thus causing the director, Ben Stoloff, to become infuriated with Tracy for stepping on his prerogatives. But Harlow never forgot Tracy's lessons and went on to become a big star.

In *She Wanted a Millionaire,* Tracy became infuriated because another newcomer, Joan Bennett (then a blonde), had all the best lines in the script. He told *The Hollywood Reporter,* "In this picture, I'm just a goddam onlooker." The trade paper, then specializing in scandal, became so intrigued with Tracy after this remark that they dug up items about his drunken brawls, his slugging a studio hand for parking in his assigned parking space, and an alleged triangle love affair involving Miss Bennett, Tracy and the film's director, John Considine. Partially as a result of all this stirred-up turmoil, plus a bad script, the picture bombed.

One of the few worthwhile pictures made by Tracy in those days was Jesse L. Lasky's *The Power and the Glory,* a review of a tycoon's tumultuous life, made after his death (and a forerunner of Orson Welles's *Citizen Kane).* He nearly blew this role because of the first of his many recorded drunken disappearances at the start of production of a film. Lasky, newly arrived at Fox from Paramount which he had helped found, had previously scheduled Tracy for a film called *Helldorado.* Lasky later wrote: "Just as *Helldorado* was ready to roll, Spence disappeared. The studio gumshoed all the bars but couldn't find him. So we had to slap Richard Arlen into the part." When a chastened Tracy showed up, about a week later, Lasky sent him off with Louise for a vacation in Hawaii "to pull yourself together." Only then, because Lasky remembered "Tracy's notable performance in *The Last Mile* on the stage," did he decide to take a chance with Tracy in the lead role of *The Power and the Glory*. The screenplay was a fine one, by Preston Sturges, and Tracy got his first fairly decent reviews since coming to Hollywood.

But his struggles at Fox continued. Edward Everett Horton, who did a dreadful picture with Tracy called *Six Cylinder Love,* recalls: "Spence had his differences with the studio, but he reacted like a rebellious child. He'd show up for work in his evening clothes, still hung over from what he was doing in them the whole night before. He was so semi-inebriated onstage once, that he even made a pass at poor little fluttery Una Merkel. Also, he developed an unreasoning hatred of the Big Red Cars."

This requires some explanation. In the Hollywood-Los Angeles growing up period, the region was crisscrossed by an ingenious network of streetcar tracks which extended into every nook and cranny of that part of Southern California. The trolleys which rode this rail system were called the Big Red Cars because of the tomato-like colour with which they were painted. You could ride them to the beach, to the mountain foothills, to downtown Los Angeles, everywhere. Los Angeles has long since regretted abandoning this near-perfect fixed-rail system in favour of building freeways.

The Big Red Cars were an important part of movie-studio operations in the 1930s. Sneak previews would be scheduled in outlying towns like

San Bernardino and Long Beach "to get the feel of real people," and stars and executives would travel in a group in a Big Red Car, instead of in their own automobiles so that, as Louis B. Mayer expressed it, "The real people would see that we're real people, too."

Tracy apparently loathed these Big Red Car preview trips, on which attendance was compulsory. Edward Everett Horton says,

"We got on the trolley for the preview of *Six Cylinder Love* at the Loyola Theater in Westchester, and Spencer was well in his cups before we even got under way. His wife, Louise, was with him, but she could not prevent him from making lascivious remarks to the pretty girls on the car, or from nipping from a hip flask he kept pulling out of his pocket. By the time the Big Red Car reached Westchester, Spencer had completely passed out. Winfield Sheehan, the head of the studio, was aboard, and he was furious."

Tracy fought incessantly with Sheehan. The scripts were bad; he wanted changes. Sheehan usually refused. Tracy accelerated his habit of disappearing for days at a time. Sheehan would organize manhunts for him all over the country, and would levy heavy fines on Tracy. Bette Davis remembers one occasion when Tracy won. She told me,

Sheehan sent a doctor friend of Tracy's to find him and to mediate. "The picture involved was, I believe, something called *Shanghai Madness*. The doctor finally located Tracy in San Francisco, as I recall, and Tracy told him, 'There's a principle involved here. The script is dishonest.' The doctor went back to Sheehan who listened, withdrew the fine against Tracy, and made the script changes he wanted."

Said James Cagney,

"Between his problems at the studio and at home, Spence was suffering a lot of pain. I remember how he went through hell in 1932 when Louise was pregnant again. He had this crazy idea that John's deafness somehow was his fault, something in his heritage, and he was terrified that the second child would be born deaf, too. There wasn't a happier guy in the world when Louise gave birth to a perfectly normal little girl, Susie."

Some of Tracy's pain in those days was relieved by his friendship with Cagney and several actors he had known in New York. They had weekly meetings and many stories have grown up about the loose society they formed. Many of the stories are incorrect. Most reports, for example, refer to the grouping as The Irishmen's Club which met unfailingly on Wednesday evenings. According to Ralph

Bellamy, one of the members, they called themselves The Boys' Club, and they met on Thursdays.

"There were seven members," says Bellamy, "Jimmy Cagney, Pat O'Brien, Frank McHugh, Frank Morgan, Lynne Overman, Tracy and myself. Not all of us were Irish, by any means. Frank Morgan, for example, was of German extraction. Anyway, we'd meet on Thursdays at various places, a back room at Chasen's or Romanoff's restaurants, our homes, a hotel suite, and we'd just drink and talk. Tracy never drank at these meetings. He was a spasmodic alcoholic."

Columnist James Bacon once asked Cagney what they talked about at the meetings. "Jimmy told me," says Bacon, "that they mulled over many serious subjects."

" 'Like what?' " I asked.

"Cagney said, 'Like we were in an upper floor room at the Beverly Hills Hotel and we spent the whole evening discussing how we'd get a coffin out of there if one of us died.' "

Tracy had other forms of release in those days. Bellamy says, "For a guy with his rough-hewn image he had some very sensitive pursuits. He was a fine art collector, for example, and once, when Cagney and I visited him, he couldn't stop talking about a quite marvellous painting he had just

bought. I seem to recall it was a Winslow Homer."
Later Tracy himself took up painting and specialized in seascapes which he sketched on stops in his
restless drives up and down the Pacific Coast High-
way. At one point, he read everything he could
about Abraham Lincoln, and committed to memory long sections of the Carl Sandburg biography.

Another example of Tracy's surprising sensitivity
was the twelve-acre ranch in Encino, in the San
Fernando Valley, where he now lived with Louise
and the two children. Says Emily Torchia, a retired
MGM publicist who knew Tracy well, "That was
the damndest farm you ever saw. That sentimental
Irishman wouldn't allow anything to be killed, not
even the chickens. So it became kind of an old-age
home for animals."

The sensitivity, and his mild demeanour in public, such as when he was with the otherwise raucous members of The Boys' Club, made his
periodic drinking binges all the more shocking. The
binges usually began when he was in revolt against
a film that Fox studio-head Sheehan wanted him to
do. Sometimes other personal pressures set him
off.

Tracy himself told me he used to like to "hide
out" at the old St. George Hotel in Brooklyn, the
most unlikely possible place for a man on the run
from Los Angeles. By carefully researching his
alcoholic escapades, and with confirmation from
Bellamy and others, I was able to piece together

the nature of the St. George excursions.

Tracy's binges usually lasted about two weeks. As he did not like to fly, he would take the Santa Fe Chief and the 20th Century Limited trains to New York (about four days) and check into the St. George, carrying a suitcase filled with whisky bottles. According to a St. George bellhop I interviewed in 1960, Tracy would lock himself in the room, strip naked and get into the bath tub. He would remain in the bathtub for a week, drinking up all the whisky, and not having to get out of the tub, not even to perform bodily functions. At the end of the week, his binge having run most of its course, he cleaned himself up, dressed, took the suitcase, now containing empty bottles, and checked out. The management of the hotel never gave away his secret, but the word leaked out from some of the employees, and even Sid Caesar told me several years later that, "I and several actors in New York knew all about Tracy in the bathtub in that hotel in Brooklyn with the swimming pool." (The St. George was noted for its large indoor pool.)

In any event, Tracy would take the train back to Los Angeles (sometimes stopping off for a few toots in Chicago, according to Ralph Bellamy), and eventually would end up on Bellamy's doorstep asking for bacon and eggs.

These escapades did not make things easier for Tracy at the studio or at home, where Louise was now doubly occupied with the lip-reading education of John and the rearing of infant Susie.

In 1933, Tracy was loaned by Fox to Columbia Pictures to do a film called *A Man's Castle,* a rather insipid romance about love in a Depression shantytown. His co-star was Loretta Young. Although she was only twenty years old, this was her thirty-sixth film, since she had begun acting professionally when she was sixteen and had been making nine or so pictures a year.

During the filming of *A Man's Castle,* the gossip columnists had a field day, reporting "an exciting new romance between Spencer Tracy and Loretta Young." As the barrage of column items continued, Tracy denied it all to an Associated Press reporter, saying, "One night, I asked Loretta to have dinner with me. I was tired of eating alone. It was just one of those things, offhand, unpremeditated. We did dine together, and the next day it cracked in the papers."

But the rumours would not go away, so Miss Young, who refuses to discuss the matter to this day, issued a flat statement: "Since Spencer Tracy and I are both Catholic and can never be married, we have agreed not to see each other again." They did, however—many times. Tracy told a reporter, "Aw, it was all platonic, anyway." To which movie star Helen Twelvetrees remarked, "When was Spence sober enough to say a thing like that?"

It is not surprising that Tracy's first separation

from Louise was announced soon after, on 29 August 1933. To take Tracy's mind off his problems, Will Rogers, also a star at Fox, induced him to concentrate on playing polo and to move into the Riviera Club, several miles to the west, on Sunset Boulevard, where the polo matches were played. Tracy had already been clandestinely playing polo with Rogers, Darryl Zanuck, Douglas Fairbanks and others, in direct defiance of his studio contract, which specifically forbade polo because of its dangers as a sport. Tracy, the rebel, got around that prohibition by playing under the rather colourful pseudonym Ivan Catchanozoff.

After a few months, Tracy tired of the constant polo at the Riviera Club, and moved into a bungalow at the Beverly Hills Hotel. He prevailed on Louise to allow him to see her and the children at weekends, while, in his off-hours during the week, he wandered up and down the coast painting his seascapes. Occasionally, he rented a boat (he later bought one), and sailed restlessly back and forth to Catalina Island. He entreated Louise to let him come back home, and, about a year after the Loretta Young incident, she relented. He moved back to their Encino ranch.

His quarrels with the studio continued. He walked out of two pictures because of script disagreements and paid a couple of his visits to his hideout at the St. George Hotel in Brooklyn. In 1934 and 1935, he made six bad pictures like

Looking for Trouble and *The Murder Man,* and only one good one, *The Show-Off,* a film version of George Kelly's Broadway hit play. In its review of Tracy's *The Show-Off, Newsweek* wrote that "the play had nearly six hundred performances on Broadway with the late Louis Bartels in the lead, and Spencer Tracy's acting compares favorably with the original." Symbolically, this picture was made by Tracy on loan-out to MGM. (Studios, in those days, made a practice of lending stars to one another for single pictures, expecting reciprocity.)

Such occasional successes as *The Show-Off* raised Tracy's spirits only temporarily. According to Ralph Bellamy, his love for his children had deepened, and he became especially close to John, who was extremely bright, and was beginning to lip-read and speak quite fluently through Louise's untiring efforts. When he was drunk, Tracy expressed these feelings in irrational ways. On 11 March 1935, he was arrested again in Yuma, Arizona, far from his studio's protection. He was charged with drunkenness, resisting an officer, and "breaking up things in a hotel room." The "things" were a complete set of dishes which he hurled around the room during a long distance phone conversation with Mrs. Tracy in Encino. The report of this incident in the *Los Angeles Times* concludes with, "the police were called and had to use force."

Apparently, this was one Tracy binge which continued for longer than usual—nearly a month.

Back from Yuma, he was doing a film called *Dante's Inferno* at Fox when one of his worst alcoholic eruptions took place. Ralph Bellamy was on the lot at the time and vividly remembers it. So did the late Jim Denton, then a publicity executive at Fox.

Said Denton:

"Tracy had been away on one of his disappearances, but he came in that morning to go to work. He was smashed out of his mind. He came roaring onto the sound stage and said he didn't like the script. He threatened the director, Harry Lachman, and chased him all around the stage. Lachman was scared to death. But then suddenly Tracy flopped down on a couch on the set and fell fast asleep. Lachman ran out and called Winfield Sheehan, the top executive at the studio. Winfield arrived and ordered the set to be evacuated — cast, crew, everyone. He then ordered the sound stage to be locked up, with the now loudly snoring Tracy inside. Sheehan's theory was that after Tracy slept it off, it would be easier to handle him.

"It didn't work out that way. Tracy woke up and began smashing things. A huge crowd gathered outside and they could hear a crash, as if someone had overturned a piece of scenery, followed by a series of explosions from

101

shattering studio lights. The demolition went on for about an hour. When Tracy finally passed out again, the studio security men went in, strait-jacketed him, and removed him. They began to total up the damage. He had pretty much wrecked the interior of the sound stage, to the tune of about a hundred thousand dollars."

Tracy was fined, eventually went back to work, and somehow finished the picture. It turned out to be one of the least distinguished efforts of his entire acting career. His co-star, Claire Trevor, said, "Usually you can connect with Spencer's eyes. That intense contact with his fellow actors is one of the major keys to his brilliance as a performer. It was missing this time."

Sheehan had had enough. It was mid-1935, the fifth year of Tracy's contract at Fox, and the contract was not renewed. He was, in short, fired. In the double-speak of the Hollywood studio system, Fox announced that, "Mr. Tracy has asked for and received his release."

Perhaps because of his fine work in *The Show-Off*, when he was on loan-out from Fox to Metro Goldwyn Mayer, Louis B. Mayer and Irving Thalberg decided to sign Tracy to an MGM contract. Thalberg later said, "It was my idea. I knew that Tracy was a fine actor who had been held back by mostly terrible movies, and we didn't make too many terrible movies at Metro. L.B. was against signing him. He said, 'We already got one drunken son-of-a-bitch to contend with — Wallace Beery. Who needs another?' But I talked him into it."

It was a fortunate change for Tracy. He had never become a major star at Fox, whose biggest money-makers were the Shirley Temple, Janet Gaynor and Will Rogers films. At Metro, he almost immediately became a box office giant, starting with *Whipsaw,* opposite Myrna Loy, and, less than a year later, making one of his finest films, the first of three with Clark Gable, *San Francisco.*

Most important of all, his switch of studios to MGM brought Katharine Hepburn into his life.

Chapter Ten

Tracy made eighteen films at MGM before he ever set eyes on Miss Hepburn. She was then under contract to RKO, across town, and Tracy did not mingle much with actors other than those who had migrated with him from Broadway.

His pre-Hepburn period in Hollywood might be termed Tracy's first Golden Age (the second Golden Age being the Hepburn-Tracy films, and the third, the pictures he made late in life with Stanley Kramer). In those first eighteen movies he did at Metro before meeting Kate, there were two Academy Awards for him, an Oscar nomination, and a couple of cult films which are still revered by students of the cinema. Between 1935 and 1942, Tracy *really* lived up to the promise he had shown in his struggling years on the stage, and in his five miserable years at Fox.

After an inauspicious start with a jewel-thief caper, *Whipsaw,* starring Myrna Loy, and another potboiler, *Riffraff*, with Jean Harlow, Tracy was rushed by Louis B. Mayer into *Fury* (now considered one of director Fritz Lang's classics). Overlapping *Fury* in production time was W. S. Van Dyke's *San Francisco*. The two films were released within three weeks of each other, early in 1936, and their critical reception was such that, almost overnight, the "promising" Tracy was a genuine movie star.

Fritz Lang was a famous German director who had escaped to the USA from the Nazis, after doing such silent masterpieces as *Metropolis*. Once ensconced at MGM, he had found a Norman Krasna script that had all the brooding violence and social significance of the great European and Russian films he had left behind. It was about a young man who is inadvertently arrested, while passing through a small town, as a suspect in a kidnapping. A terrifying sequence ensues in which a lynch mob is formed and burns down the jail. The young man, Joe Wilson, played by Tracy, is supposed dead, but escapes to track down his would-be killers, causing them to be brought to trial for his murder. He shows up at the trial, just as the death sentence is about to be pronounced, and delivers a memorable speech about lynch-law and compassion. It is a confusing ending but a marvellous opportunity for an actor of Tracy's capabilities.

It is not known why Lang chose Tracy from among the many MGM stars available to him, but Tracy took on the role, even though, as usual, he hated the script. He later said, "I remembered that I also hated the script of *The Last Mile,* and look what a powerful hunk of drama *that* turned out to be. I figured that *Fury* maybe had some of the same kind of elements in it. But I thought it wouldn't make a nickel at the box-office."

Despite the dominance of the male protagonist in the Krasna story, the star of *Fury* was Sylvia Sidney, who played Joe Wilson's fiancee. Tracy got second billing to her. He fought constantly with Lang over the director's Teutonic meticulousness and obsessiveness about working late hours, and was glad to escape to the overlapping production of *San Francisco*, where things were wide open.

San Francisco, of course, was the first time he worked with Clark Gable. Gable was the star of the film; Jeanette MacDonald was the co-star; Tracy only got third billing. Director W. S. Van Dyke, already famous for his *Trader Horn* and *The Thin Man,* had sensed a weakness in the Anita Loos script about the romance between a San Francisco bar-owner (Gable) and a would-be opera singer (MacDonald) who get caught up in the 1906 San Francisco earthquake. There was a secondary character, a priest named Father Mullin who is a close friend of the bar-owner, and Van Dyke wanted the role of the priest built up to give the story "more power and humanity." Van Dyke had been watching Tracy's work on the stage, and in some of his less dreadful films.

Van Dyke requested Tracy. He got him, although Tracy later said, "I had a tough time deciding whether or not to get myself out of the part. I thought of how my father wanted me to be a priest, and I wondered if it would be sacrilegious for me to *play* a priest. All of my Catholic training and background rolled around in my head, but then I figured Dad would have liked it, and I threw myself into the role."

In the middle of production, on 4 December 1935, Tracy threw himself into a bit of relaxation at the Trocadero night club and got into a fist fight on the dance floor with director William Wellman. This was *not* one of Tracy's pugilistic triumphs. He was drunk, and his fists did not respond as readily as they had when he was a boy in Milwaukee. He was flattened by Wellman, and suffered a spectacular-looking black eye. The story of the brawl was reported in all the Los Angeles papers.

MGM boss Mayer was furious, and, according to Irving Thalberg, said, "I *told* you he was a trouble-maker from what he used to do at Fox." Thalberg dissuaded Mayer from firing Tracy on the spot, saying, "We could handle Wallace Beery, so we could handle *him*."

A few weeks later, Mayer's ire turned to glee when both *Fury* and *San Francisco* opened in New York. The critics raved about *Fury*, and declared Tracy a dramatic star of the magnitude of Paul Muni. Concerning *San Francisco,* Frank Nugent wrote in the *New York Times*, "Mr. Tracy, late of *Fury*, is heading surely toward an award for the finest performance of the year." Hailed as a masterpiece, slightly flawed because of its ambiguous ending, *Fury* went on to become a hit among the art-house moviegoers, while *San Francisco* became a hit *everywhere,* a genuine box-office bonanza. Tracy got the Academy Award nomination for best actor, not the film's star, Gable. But, ironically, Paul Muni won the Oscar that year for *The Story of Louis Pasteur*.

No matter. Tracy suddenly had become one of MGM's biggest money-makers, and he was immediately cast in *Libeled Lady,* with three of MGM's other big money-makers, William Powell, Myrna Loy and Jean Harlow. The *Libeled Lady* set was a madhouse, with reporters swarming in to watch all that Hollywood royalty together on one sound stage. Tracy, unused to so much concentrated attention from the press, snapped and snarled, and soaked the seat of one overly persistent reporter's pants by forcibly causing him to sit in a urinal in the men's room.

Powell and Loy, who had done many films together, generally hung out by themselves. Tracy spent most of his time with Harlow who, since he had first coached her in *Goldie* at Fox, had done such important films as *Red Dust, Dinner at Eight* and *Bombshell*. Tracy had already worked with her at MGM in *Riffraff,* but that was a quickie schedule, and there had not been much time to gossip. And gossip was one thing Tracy always loved. Married three times, with one of her husbands, MGM executive Paul Bern, committing suicide in apparent despair over his sexual impotence, Harlow had plenty of personal gossip to dispense. She seems to have done so with great vigour—while creating even more gossip. At least twice, she was photographed in intimate huddled conversation with Tracy at the Trocadero.

Tracy loved doing *Libeled Lady,* which was a farce similar to many he had done on the stage. His very next picture, however, was a total departure from farce. Irving Thalberg came on the set of *Libeled Lady* one day, told Tracy that he was one of the finest actors in films, and then added nonchalantly, "We're thinking of you for *Captains Courageous.*"

As was customary with his finest work, Tracy had doubts about the great Rudyard Kipling classic from the very beginning. He brooded a lot about it when he was cast in the film. He complained that, "it was the boy's picture" (the boy being Freddie Bartholomew, playing Harvey Cheyne), and that the part of Manuel, the Portuguese fisherman, had been a comparatively minor character in Kipling's original work. He was not even convinced after reading the script and seeing that the role of Manuel had been built up considerably. It took the director, Victor Fleming, whom Tracy admired, to stimulate his interest in the project, by saying, "This is going to be a great film, and we're all going to be proud for having been a part of it."

Louise Tracy, too, sensed the importance of the picture, just as she had with *The Last Mile.* Tracy's relationship with Louise at that time was confusing. He was living with her at their Encino ranch, but he seems to have been spending many of his nights elsewhere, such as the Beverly Hills Hotel, or his brother Carroll's house. This puzzled his friends, James Cagney among them, who said, "We didn't know what was going on with Spence and Louise. One night he'd show up at Romanoff's restaurant with her; then he'd show up with one of the starlets from MGM, Judy Garland, for example, who then was only fifteen."

The uncertainty in his marriage matched the insecurity he always had shown in his work. At the time of *Captains Courageous,* his salary had been raised to five thousand dollars a week (closing in on Gable's $6,500 a week), but as Louise told writer J. P. McEvoy, "During the entire time we've been married, I've never known Spence to be without fear of the future, a continual fear that any minute now they're going to 'catch on to him' and all this money is going to stop, that he's going to turn out to be just one of those flashes in the pan."

Concerning his specific trepidations about *Captains Courageous,* Tracy said,

"I worried that I'd look like a dope when they curled my hair for the part of Manuel, and it didn't help any when Joan Crawford yelled from her car on the lot one day, 'Hey, look who's here. It's Harpo Marx.' Then I worried about learning a Portuguese accent. I had never done *any* accent before. But I researched how people from Portugal talk when they come to the U.S. of A., and I thought I had the problem licked. But then the studio brought in a real Portuguese-American fisherman, and I sat down in Victor Fleming's office to talk to him. I said, 'Now how would you say leetle feesh?' and he said, 'I'd say little fish.' "

Much later, Tracy confessed to writer Abby Mann that he gave up then and there, deciding to use what was mostly a Yiddish accent, with which he had become familiar in his New York theatre days. It did not seem to matter. In the naive Hollywood of the 1930s, a foreign accent was a foreign accent, as Samuel Goldwyn once put it, when casting a Polish actor to play a Frenchman.

In any event, the filming of *Captains Courageous,* once it started, went fairly smoothly, except for a brief pause in the filming when Tracy had "pneumonia" (this may have been the interlude when he got drunk at the Beverly Wilshire Hotel and tried to hurl his brother, Carroll, out of the window). In all, director Fleming was pleased with Tracy's performance. Said Fleming,

"Spence was overwhelmed at working with his old idol, Lionel Barrymore, and kept trying to show the old man just what he was capable of. Spence also liked the kid, Freddie Bartholomew, and called him a real performer, the only child actor he ever knew who didn't try to be cute. I even got Spence to sing and play the Portuguese musical instrument called the vielle. He has no voice at all, and his singing was terrible, but it was just right because Manuel's singing would have been terrible, too."

Much of the picture was shot off the coast of California (doubling for the Grand Banks of Newfoundland). Fleming used an authentic Gloucester schooner, the *We're Here,* and Tracy annoyed the captain of the vessel by wanting to take the helm between shots. "I'm practising," he said, "because I'm in negotiations to buy my own ketch, which I'm going to name the *Carrie B.,* after my mother." The captain could not have cared less, and, according to Victor Fleming, had forcibly to remove Tracy from the bridge when a sudden Pacific storm came up. Tracy's final drowning scene was a trial to Fleming, and had to be done over and over again.

Said Fleming, "The son-of-a-bitch, whom I love, kept trying to make the sign of the cross, which wasn't in the script, and it's hard to do that while you're treading water. He took on so much water that we had to attach a line to him to keep him from drowning *himself.* He's a stubborn bastard, but he was right. The take we used in the picture was just great."

When the film was completed, Tracy still wasn't sure it was any good. Disconsolate, he rushed into his next picture, *They Gave Him a Gun,* with Franchot Tone. He was still saying, "I was positive I had done the worst job of my life," when *Captains Courageous* was released to unanimous rave reviews, typical of which was *Time Magazine's:* "[it] offers its credentials for admission to the thin company of cinema immortals."

Even then, Tracy had no idea of how his performance in *Fury, San Francisco* and now, *Captains Courageous,* had won him the adulation of the world's film audiences. He took a trip to Cuba, the first time he had been out of the Los Angeles area since he moved to MGM from Fox. In Havana, a mob of reporters met him at the boat; he was overwhelmed by thousands of fans when he descended to the dock. Frightened and annoyed, he booked himself on the next ship back to the United States.

Once again, Tracy won the Academy Award nomination ahead of the actor who had received top billing, Freddie Bartholomew.

The Awards dinner was held on 10 March 1938, at the Ambassador Hotel in Los Angeles. Tracy was not present. His health had begun to deteriorate. He was in hospital for a hernia operation, but he also had throat and thyroid problems. So Louise Tracy went alone to the Oscar ceremonies.

When Tracy was announced as Best Actor for his performance in *Captains Courageous,* Louise, with great dignity, ascended the podium to accept the statuette on his behalf. She made one of the shortest speeches in Academy history: "I thank you for Spencer, Johnnie, Susie and myself, and I want to tell all of you how much all of us appreciate it." The crowd, most of whom had never seen Louise before, and who had been reading rumours that the Tracy marriage was on the verge of dissolution, erupted into tumultuous applause.

Then came an impromptu Louis B. Mayer speech which raised eyebrows throughout the ballroom: "I'd like to praise Spencer Tracy's sense of discipline. Tracy is a fine actor, but he is most important because he understands why it is necessary to take orders from the front office."

One of the orders had been to stop riding horses, because Tracy had become prone to falling off them. Another of the orders had been to co-operate in writing the Tracy autobiographical series for his hometown newspaper, the *Milwaukee Sentinel,* and to make it all sweetness and light.

In the final instalment of the series, on 6 February 1937, Tracy declared, "If there has been any change for the better in my life and in my work in the last year, it is due solely and completely to Mrs. Tracy. My wife is the finest, most loyal woman I ever hope to know."

Chapter Eleven

After seeing Tracy's Oscar-winning performance in *Captains Courageous,* Katharine Hepburn, still at RKO, spoke with her close friend, writer-director Garson Kanin. She told Kanin, "I don't know this man, but he has enormous power, versatility and masculinity as an actor. I'd like to do a picture with him some day." Kanin knew Tracy and passed this information on to him. It seems, from what Kanin wrote later, that Tracy only grunted disinterestedly.

Tracy's career was then moving ahead at breakneck speed — *Big City* and *Mannequin* (neither of them particularly distinguished), and then, later, in 1938, his second film with Gable and director Victor Fleming, *Test Pilot*. This was the cliché-ridden flying film which Sid Caesar later savagely satirized in his so-called aeroplane routine, even down to Tracy, the mechanic, sticking his chewing gum on the plane's fuselage for luck, while Gable, the pilot, careened nonchalantly through the hazardous skies.

Tracy was not entirely happy with *Test Pilot*. He said "I was getting tired of being the good-guy schnook while Gable had all the scenes with the girl" (in this case, Myrna Loy). Gable was once again overwhelmed with Tracy's innate acting talent, and called him "the best in the business, bar none." Gable was none too bright, however, and fell easy prey to Tracy's predilection to needle and to cause mischief when bored. Tracy, for example, used all his actor's tricks to delay his death after a plane crash which, realistically, should have killed him instantly. Finally, Gable complained to Fleming, "The son-of-a-bitch is a slower dier than Cagney. At the rate he's going, it's gonna take him four reels to kick off."

Slow-dying or not, the film was another big box-office hit, and Tracy made sure that in his third, and last, film with Gable, *Boom Town,* in 1940, he got equal billing, equal time in the wildcat oil-field action, and even one of the girls, Hedy Lamarr.

But first came another Tracy masterpiece—a far cry from the Gable-Tracy buddy pictures which made money, had spectacular special effects, but were hardly landmarks of great film acting. Tracy's last picture in 1938 was *Boys Town*. Again, he was to play a priest, the real-life Father Edward J. Flanagan, and again he went through the turmoil of guilt about not having become a priest himself. He resolved his doubts when he met the quiet, dignified, forceful Rev. Flanagan who had founded the famous institution for wayward youths in Nebraska, on his theory that "there are no bad boys".

Tracy spent some time with Father Flanagan in Omaha, and later wrote, "He's a great man—the greatest man I ever met." As this was to be the first living person he ever played, he resolved to play him exactly as he was, with no actor's tricks. For his part, the famous priest couldn't have been more delighted. Earlier, when MGM had asked him what actor he would most want to play him, he had said, "Spencer Tracy, without any question."

For once, Tracy began a film with no doubts in his mind. He got along passably well with his co-star, Mickey Rooney, then only seventeen years old, and always spoke highly of him.

Rooney played Whitey Marsh, an incorrigible youth who is tamed by Father Flanagan after much suffering and ends up as Mayor of Boys Town. The film had a mushy ending, with Whitey and Father Flanagan helping to corral some criminals, and saving Boys Town from financial disaster with the reward money they receive (probably a Louis B. Mayer sob-story touch, to which the MGM tsar was habitually partial).

The filming went off without any untoward incidents. Tracy behaved himself, and seemed genuinely enthralled with the subject matter. Henry Hull, playing the other important adult in the cast, said,

"We had a technical adviser on the set, a young Catholic priest, name of Father John O'Donnell, and Spence spent a lot of time with him talking about a lot of church stuff I didn't understand. But I remember one argument they had about who was who at the Last Supper, and Spence was using baseball lingo to describe the Apostles—like 'Andrew was a singles hitter but Peter was a guy who could play clean-up and knock the ball out of the park.' I don't remember Spence getting particularly close to any of the boys, including Rooney, but he put on the boxing gloves with the bigger kids one day, just fooling around, and one kid jabbed Spence's head off, and Spence got mad. Rooney was a lot like Spence. He kept to himself and they didn't have much truck with each other off-camera."

When the film was released, there was general agreement that Tracy had never been better. The *New York Times* critic, Frank Nugent, wrote, "Spencer Tracy's performance of Father Flanagan is perfection itself." Stanley Kramer, who much later produced and directed four Tracy films, made an interesting comment to me about *Boys Town*. Said Kramer,

"I rank the Father Flanagan role as one of

Spence's greatest. It wasn't a performance, it wasn't an interpretation. You might say it was a *feeling* of the man that he unerringly imparted. You knew that Father Flanagan was torn, the way Spence played him. The priest could be just as tough as the kid he was trying to help, yet he could retreat not only to being a man of great humanity, but also a messenger from God, in a sense."

Kramer, of course, did not know of Tracy's inner turmoil about not having become a priest in real life, and yet he was saying, in effect, that Tracy was playing Father Flanagan as if he, Tracy, *were* a real priest.

Once again, the over-sentimental ending notwithstanding, *Boys Town* was a super-blockbuster at the box-office. The Oscar competition became a two-man race between Tracy and his old friend, Cagney, who made *Angels With Dirty Faces* that same year. Tracy won. He became the only man in history to be awarded Best Actor Oscars in consecutive years.

Tracy was at the peak of his fame, but didn't know how to handle it. He went to Europe with Louise, but provoked another mob scene at the first stop, Waterloo Station in London. Thousands of his fans trampled each other in the rush to catch a glimpse of him (Arturo Toscanini, an innocent bystander, was one of those trampled).

"We were unprepared for the crowds at the platform that met the boat train," said Louise. "We waited for everyone to get off, thinking we could sneak out some way, but the crowds wouldn't move, so the train had to back up to another station to let us off. More crowds, people jammed together, knocking each other down. This scared Spencer so, he started talking immediately about coming home."

In all, Tracy was thoroughly miserable on the trip, even when the crowds subsided. He was barely civil to the press, but they wrote glowing stories about him, anyway.

Not long after their return to Los Angeles, Tracy decided he wanted to spend some time in New York to see some plays. Mostly he saw the bar at the Lambs Club, where he spent nearly every night roistering, while Louise remained alone back at their hotel. He was dead drunk, passed out in the club, when he and Louise were to take the train back home. Louise was called, but did not come to get him. His friends at the club had to lug him back to his hotel, just in time to make the train.

Tracy had more time on his hands now because he was a superstar and the studio was devoting a lot of effort to finding just the right screen properties for his specialized talents. Irving Thalberg was gone, demoted in 1933, and dead, at the age of thirty-seven, in 1936, so Louis B. Mayer was making all the decisions. The Mayer decisions were not always acceptable to Tracy.

A sequel to *Boys Town,* called *Men of Boys Town,* was only a shadow of its original; *I Take This Woman,* personally produced by Mayer for his new favourite, Hedy Lamarr, was ridiculed by the critics. This teaming of Tracy with Lamarr was notable for one of Tracy's more whimsical on-stage needling pranks. As he told writer Abby Mann years later, he did not like Hedy. He thought she was taking advantage of her closeness to Mayer, and putting on airs of being overly prim. Says Mann, "Spence told me, 'I thought I'd fix Hedy one day. We had a scene where she had to sit on my lap. The night before we did the scene, I bought a big banana that wasn't ripe yet and was pretty hard. I slipped the banana down the front of my pants, and when Hedy sat down on it, she let out a scream and jumped about ten fuckin' feet in the air.' "

Despite the feuding (and the creaming by the critics) *I Take This Woman* made money for MGM, probably because of Tracy and his continuing name value. The same was true of an epic, *Northwest Passage,* conceived as another *Gone With the Wind* by Louis B. Mayer. The film took a year to get into production, and when it began, late in the summer of 1939, four of its original stars, Robert Taylor, Franchot Tone, Wallace Beery and Greer Garson, were dispersed to other projects. Only Tracy remained of the previously announced cast. He was joined by Robert Young, who loved the physically arduous locations in the rugged Cascade Mountains of Oregon. Tracy, normally a more sedentary type, hated them. He complained that "I wore out a pair of fuckin' leather pants just in one fuckin' river crossing." He did, however, get on well with Young, and with Walter Brennan, who was more like his own fractious self.

Northwest Passage was the setting for one of Tracy's more famous bon mots. When director King Vidor sought to hire a band of local Indians as extras, and the Indians demanded ten dollars apiece per day, Tracy said, "Tell the fuckers they'll be working as half-breeds, so they'll only be worth five dollars a day."

When *Northwest Passage* was released in 1940, Tracy got the kudos from the critics, but the picture did not.

Tracy was getting restless again. There were no big boozing episodes during this period, but he seemed to go into a frenzy of extra-marital dating on his nights away from home. He was seen with Judy Garland in night spots, and also with Olivia De Havilland, duly reported in the fan magazines, with photos. Once, Pat O'Brien spotted him in intimate conversation with Marlene Dietrich in an out of the way little restaurant in the San Fernando

Valley. O'Brien said to Tracy, "What are *you* doing here?" To which (O'Brien reported) Miss Dietrich replied, "We're discussing wired bras, darling."

There were only two films which Tracy liked in these troubled latter days of his first Golden Age. One was *Edison the Man,* about the struggles of inventor Thomas Edison. The other was *Stanley and Livingstone,* which he made for Darryl Zanuck, on loan-out to 20th Century-Fox. This picture exhilarated him, he said, because "what a pleasure it was to work with such a fine actor, Sir Cedric Hardwicke" (who played the lost African missionary Dr. David Livingstone to Tracy's searching news reporter, Henry Stanley).

Tracy's first Golden Age ended in a thump in 1941, with the release of a picture which was possibly his worst performance ever. Some of the deep thinkers at MGM had come up with the idea of a remake of Robert Louis Stevenson's *Dr. Jekyll and Mr. Hyde,* which had won an Oscar for Fredric March at Paramount in 1932. Louis B. Mayer bought the idea; Tracy resisted it at first, saying, "Who could top Freddie's performance? And why would anyone want to try?"

The moguls kept after Tracy, however, and he began to contemplate an interesting concept for the picture. Perhaps thinking of his own dual personae, as a Jekyll when sober and a Hyde when drunk, he proposed to MGM executive Eddie Mannix that the story be done as a lesson in how alcohol and drugs can bring out the evil side of a man. Mannix said,

"It was an interesting idea to me, but Mr. Mayer wouldn't go for it. He wanted to do it straight, with Dr. Jekyll mixing the mysterious potion in his own laboratory, and then changing into Mr. Hyde whenever he drank it. Mr. Mayer thought that if Spence flipped out when he drank booze and took dope, it would be too close to home for a lot of people, and besides, it would make a 'message picture', which L.B. hated."

Tracy grumbled, but agreed to do the film, mostly because his old friend Victor Fleming was to produce and direct it. He also became intrigued with the idea that two exciting female newcomers were in the supporting cast, Lana Turner as the girl he loved when he was Dr. Jekyll, and Ingrid Bergman as the barmaid he lusted after when he was the evil Mr. Hyde.

An immediate problem for director Fleming was that Tracy had to wear make-up, which he always hated throughout his acting career. The second problem was that the make-up did not work. Unlike Fredric March, an extremely handsome man, Tracy's craggy countenance did not vary that much from Jekyll to Hyde, causing visitors to the set to ask, "Which is he playing now, the good guy or the bad guy?"

A third problem was that Tracy developed a personal relationship with Bergman during the filming, which did not help Fleming in his directing of them, since Fleming's love letters to Ingrid later revealed that he, too, had been having a serious affair with her. This led to occasional flare-ups between Fleming and Tracy, normally very good friends. One time, for example, Fleming insisted that Tracy hoist Bergman over his shoulder and carry her up a steep flight of stairs to a bedroom. To demonstrate, and to show off his own physical fitness at fifty-eight, Fleming picked up the rather large Bergman, flung her over *his* shoulder and carried her up the stairs. In a heated conversation out of Ingrid's earshot, Tracy, according to Donald Crisp, who was standing nearby, said, "Goddamit, she's too fuckin' big and heavy for me. You'll have to use some kind of a sling to lift her up and keep her there while I carry her." After a long, bitter argument Fleming acceded and they used the sling.

Actor-director John Houseman was on the set frequently, and says, "I watched Ingrid's growing relationship with Spencer, but that's not uncommon in this business." Tracy's close personal friend Billy Grady, also later confirmed the fact of a Tracy-Bergman affair. So, in effect, did Bergman's husband, Dr. Petter Lindstrom, who says that months after *Jekyll and Hyde* he refused to allow Ingrid to go off to San Francisco for two weeks "to discuss future roles".

As for Tracy, he said, "Aw, the only thing Ingrid and I did was to have hamburgers and milkshakes every day at a drive-in in Beverly Hills."

With all these currents and crosscurrents, it is not surprising that *Dr. Jekyll and Mr. Hyde* was creamed by the critics. And so, too, was Tracy, for one of the few times in his life. Theodore Strauss wrote in the *New York Times,* "Tracy's portrait of Hyde is not so much evil incarnate as it is the ham incarnate . . . When his eyes roll in a fine frenzy, like loose marbles in his head, he is more ludicrous than dreadful . . . Only Miss Bergman has emerged with some measure of honor."

This was only Ingrid's fourth American film. She moved on to do the memorable *Casablanca* with Humphrey Bogart. The distraught Tracy, consoled by the fact that *Dr. Jekyll and Mr. Hyde* did well financially, moved on to another disaster. This time, however, he could not take the blame.

The movie was *The Yearling,* another long-planned Louis B. Mayer epic. Filming began in the Everglades in Florida, with King Vidor directing. Tracy was excited about working with the skilled actress Anne Revere, whom he had spotted on the stage and who had been in the *Boys Town* sequel, *Men of Boys Town.* But the picture was not to be. Beset by hordes of insects, deplorable working conditions, and a change of directors from Vidor to Victor Fleming, Mayer cancelled the film com-

A rare photograph of Spencer Tracy with his wife, Louise. (Kobal Collection)

With his son, John and daughter, Susie. (National Film Archive)

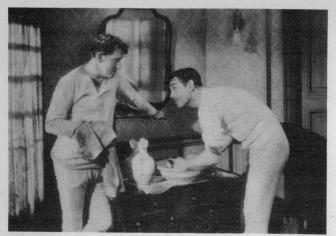

Clark Gable starring with Tracy in *Boom Town*. (Kobal Collection)

Boys Town. (National Film Archive)

Above: Spencer Tracy teamed with Katharine Hepburn for the first time in *Woman of the Year,* and *below,* seven years later in *Adam's Rib.* (Kobal Collection)

On and off set in *Father of the Bride*. (Kobal Collection and
National Film Archive)

With Elizabeth Taylor in *Father's Little Dividend*. (Kobal
Collection)

Dr. Jekyll and Mr. Hyde. (Kobal Collection)

Face to face with Ernest Hemingway during the filming of *The Old Man and the Sea*. (National Film Archive)

Judgment at Nuremberg. Left: The opening scene and *below* with (from left) director Stanley Kramer and co-stars Burt Lancaster, Judy Garland, Spencer Tracy, Richard Widmark and Maximillian Schell. (The Photo Source)

On screen together for the last time, Tracy and Hepburn in *Guess Who's Coming to Dinner*. (Kobal Collection)

Relaxing in the studio between rehearsals of *Guess Who's Coming to Dinner.* (Kobal Collection)

pletely after six weeks of fruitless struggle in the Everglades.

The project was to be revived again, five years later, with Gregory Peck and Jane Wyman.

In 1941, Tracy returned from Florida in one of his depressive states. He was a failure, another of those flashes in the pan, perhaps he would never work again, perhaps he should try to find some other way of earning a living.

This was when Katharine Hepburn finally came into his life, and it couldn't have been at a more opportune time.

Chapter Twelve

It's an oft-told tale, but the essential facts bear repeating. Katharine Hepburn had gone to RKO in 1932, following her Broadway triumph in *The Warrior's Husband* in 1932. She had never crossed paths with Tracy in New York because she was nine years younger and moved in a much higher-class social set. She had quickly made her mark at RKO, winning the Best Actress Oscar for *Morning Glory,* in 1933, just one year after she arrived. But she had had an up and down, sometimes personal, relationship with RKO's eccentric boss, Howard Hughes, and bought her way out of her studio contract in 1938.

With a string of mostly good pictures behind her (*Little Women, Alice Adams, Stage Door*), she had then returned to Broadway for the Philip Barry play *The Philadelphia Story,* an enormous stage hit, adored by both the critics and the public. A shrewd business woman, and wise to the ways of Hollywood, she had arranged in advance with playwright Barry to option the film rights to his play. So, when Louis B. Mayer bought *The Philadelphia Story* for an MGM movie, Miss Hepburn came along as part of the package. He had to agree to her insistence that she be the female star of the film.

With George Cukor as the director and Cary Grant and James Stewart as Hepburn's co-stars, *The Philadelphia Story* became one of the best films ever made in Hollywood, winning an Oscar for Stewart. Hepburn, who had been signed to a one-picture deal only, was now in a position to negotiate seriously with Mayer for a long-term MGM contract. She had also begun to look around for screen properties for herself. And, harking back to her admiration of Tracy in *Captains Courageous* she reminded Garson Kanin of her desire to do a film with Tracy, whom she had still never met.

In 1941, while Tracy was embroiled in his *Dr. Jekyll and Mr. Hyde* fiasco (which, by the way, Miss Hepburn later wrote that she liked), a young writer, Ring Lardner Jr, came to Kanin with a screenplay about his father, the famous humorist and short-story writer, Ring Lardner. The story focused on the elder Lardner's tempestuous relationship with the celebrated political columnist, Dorothy Thompson.

Kanin had liked the concept and brought in his

younger brother, Michael Kanin, to rewrite the script with Lardner Jr. The screenplay, *Woman of the Year,* evolved into the story of the tempestuous relationship between a sportswriter, Sam Craig, and pundit-columnist Tess Harding, who worked on the same New York newspaper. Sam and Tess fussed and feuded all the way into marriage, and then *almost* out of it again.

Hepburn loved the script when Kanin showed it to her. She stormed into Louis B. Mayer's office, saying, in effect, "This is the picture I want to do — with Spencer Tracy." Since Kanin was going into World War II military service, she also insisted on George Stevens (whom she had dated) as the director. After reading the script, Mayer capitulated, for one of the few times in his life. She demanded the odd sum of $211,000 for the property, which included $100,000 for herself and $100,000 for the two comparatively unknown young writers. Mayer grumbled and said yes, but she would have to wait for Tracy to finish *The Yearling.* The Florida insects terminated *The Yearling* soon thereafter, and Tracy was suddenly available.

The first meeting between Tracy and Hepburn became an apocryphal story which was printed and reprinted for years. She is supposed to have said, "I fear I may be too tall for you, Mr. Tracy." (She is 5ft 9½in in high heels; Tracy was a little less than 5ft 10in.) Tracy's alleged reply was,

"Don't worry. I'll cut you down to my size." In 1986, Hepburn finally set the record straight. It was not a formally arranged confrontation, as had been reported, but a chance encounter on the steps of the Thalberg Building at MGM, where they were introduced by their mutual friend, director Joe Mankiewicz. It was Mankiewicz, *not* Tracy, who said, *"He'll* cut you down to size."

In any event, according to writer Michael Kanin, "Kate and Spence fell into a wonderful, natural working relationship after just a few days of sparring on the set. It was easier for Kate. She had known men like Spence before. Like all the rest of us, Spence had never known anyone like Kate."

Who had? She was ahead of her time, a patrician-born, extremely bright, independent young woman, who was an early advocate of women's rights, a political radical, and a constant rebel against what she called the inanities of the Hollywood system. The obvious symbol of her rebellion, of course, was her habit of wearing rumpled pants or overalls, when tailored skirts and dresses were *de rigueur* for nearly all other film and stage actresses.

Kate was born in Hartford, Connecticut, one of the six children of Dr. Thomas Norval Hepburn, a surgeon-urologist who was one of the Hepburns of Virginia, and Katharine Houghton Hepburn, one of the Houghtons of Boston. Dr. Hepburn's ancestry went all the way back to the Court of Mary

Queen of Scots; Mrs. Hepburn had a cousin who was the US Ambassador to Great Britain. Both were descendants of early settlers in colonial America—and remember how impressed Tracy was over the fact that his mother, Carrie, was one of the Browns of Rhode Island, and that Louise's Episcopalian family had deep roots in Pennsylvania.

Dr. Hepburn was a rare political liberal among his ultraconservative medical confreres. Mrs. Hepburn was even more of a hell-raiser in her aristocratic New England set. She was a suffragette and a crusader for birth control. She picketed the White House for better working conditions for women. She used the Hepburns' elegant beach home, Fenwick, for a benefit affair to raise funds for hungry Indian children. Fenwick, and the Hepburns' city mansion in West Hartford, were the scenes of almost constant intellectual discussion among all members of the family. "No argument was finished," said Kate, "until everyone had had his or her say." All this was totally new to Tracy, and it fascinated him.

Kate went to Bryn Mawr, the elite women's college. When she graduated she could have gone on to medical school, like her father, but drama had intrigued her more, and she began her acting career in a theatre stock company in Baltimore. At nineteen, she married Ludlow Ogden Smith, a Philadelphia socialite. She lived with Luddie, as she called him, in a cramped little apartment on East 39th Street in New York, for a little more than two weeks, because she could not stand "having to worry about taking care of another person's needs." They separated, but remained good friends until their formal divorce, several years later.

Then came more acting in stock, her successes on Broadway and in Hollywood, leading up to her teaming with Tracy in *Woman of the Year* when he was forty-one years old and she not yet thirty-two.

Production went smoothly on *Woman of the Year,* although one unverifiable published account states that Tracy staged one of his disappearances halfway through the film, and that Hepburn scoured Los Angeles to find him, took him home, and sobered him up. Writer Michael Kanin says, "The magic between the two was evident on the sound stage. Maybe that's because the way we wrote the script, the characters of Sam Craig and Tess Harding were very much how we saw Spence and Kate in real life, the gruff, cantankerous but loving male and the wise accommodating female who ends up getting her own way." There was even a monumental drunk scene for Tracy in the script.

When it was released, in 1942, *Woman of the Year* was an enormous success. Most critics rhapsodized about "the magic" generated on the screen by Tracy and Hepburn. The magic continued into their next film, *Keeper of the Flame,* which, again, was about a journalist. This time, Tracy meets up with Hepburn, the widow of a national leader, whose puzzling car-crash death Tracy is investigating.

The magic also continued into the personal lives of Tracy and Hepburn. As Michael Kanin told me, "It was obvious to everyone on the sound stage that they had fallen in love while working together in *Woman of the Year."*

The open question is, "Why did Hepburn fall in love with him, with all his problems?" Perhaps she thought she alone could save him, a noble compulsion not unknown to psychiatrists. Their closest friend, director George Cukor, expressed this theory to me much later on.

Certainly, Hepburn was impressed with Tracy's overt virility and masculinity in a theatrical and film world populated with many homosexuals. In explaining their success on the screen together, she told writer Roy Newquist,

Certainly the ideal American man is Spencer. Sports-loving, a man's man. Strong looking, a big sort of head, boar neck, and so forth. A man. And I think I represent a woman. I needle him, and I irritate him, and I try to get around him, yet if he put a big paw out, he could squash me. I think this is the sort of romantic ideal picture of the male and female in the United States."

Was it also the sort of romantic ideal picture of Tracy and Hepburn together in their own personal lives? George Cukor thought so.

Certainly, Hepburn was impressed with Tracy's innate talent. She said, without equivocation to Newquist, "He is the most remarkable actor ever born."

But there are more subtle hints to the depths of their relationship. In 1986, Kate wrote an article for *TV Guide* in which she discussed Tracy's original idea for his failed *Dr. Jekyll and Mr. Hyde* film, the idea that was rejected by the studio. As Tracy explained it to her, Jekyll had a lovely, very proper fiancee, while Hyde "either because of drink or dope or who knows what" would perform "incredible acts of cruelty and vulgarity" with a whore in another neighbourhood. Kate wrote that Tracy wanted the fiancee and the whore to be played by the same actress, and that "I was the girl he had in mind," even though "at this time we had never met."

Miss Hepburn mused in the article, "Later I wondered why he had happened to light upon this notion for *Jekyll and Hyde*. Was there some personal connotation?"

Earlier on, this question also puzzled their good friend, George Cukor. He said to me, "Did Spence want the good and the bad in a woman to match the good and the bad in *him?* If so, why Kate? How much badness could anyone find in Kate?"

Chapter Thirteen

By now, Tracy was seeing less and less of his wife, Louise, although friends say he telephoned nearly every day and saw his two children frequently. Kenneth Leffers, a veteran bellhop at the Beverly Hills Hotel, says that, when a new wing was completed, Tracy moved permanently into Room 491, a top-floor corner suite. It was Hepburn's habit to play tennis early every morning with the hotel's pro—"sometimes even mopping up the court with towels after a rain" says Leffers—and then have breakfast with Tracy.

Louise Tracy said to a reporter, around that time, "I have to read the Hollywood trade papers to find out what Spencer is doing in his work." Yet, as far as the world at large knew, he was still living at home and helping Louise in her career, dedicated to the needs of deaf children and their parents.

It was just about when Tracy was filming

Woman of the Year that Louise founded the now world-famous John Tracy Clinic. The year was 1942, and John, then eighteen years old, had learned to lip-read and to speak, because of the unceasing efforts of his mother. He was quite a good student in school, though he had had to catch up because of his impairment, but it had been tough work for Louise, who had consulted with the leading otologists in the world. Because John was "nerve-deaf," no hearing aid could help him. Louise said,

"The first time I knew he'd ever be able to 'hear' with his eyes and eventually speak, was when he was about two years old. He was lying in bed, making child sounds. He looked at me, not at my eyes, but at my mouth. I said, 'Mama, mama.' He took about a second and then silently copied what he saw, with his mouth. That was the first step toward lip-reading, and the clinic."

The clinic began after Louise, who had been speaking about the problems of rearing deaf children at luncheons and teas, took part in a panel discussion at the University of Southern California, and got to meet Dr. Rufus B. von KleinSmid, USC's president. Soon thereafter Dr. KleinSmid offered her the use of a small decrepit building on the campus. Louise, and her friends, and some

USC students, put the building back into repair, and the John Tracy Clinic was formally opened in September 1942. The clinic quickly grew to an enrolment of twenty mothers and hearing-impaired children, and Dr. KleinSmid had to offer two more buildings— temporary wartime structures—to the enterprise, which was incorporated, in 1943, with Walt Disney and Spencer Tracy on its original five-person board of directors. Louise was President and Director-in-charge.

Louise wisely gathered together groups of lady auxiliaries, mostly from among the area's upper-crust socialites. Among them was Mrs. Jessie Blakiston, daughter of the owner of *The Baltimore Sun*. Mrs. Blakiston, who served as a board member of the clinic for more than thirty years, told me:

"Louise was one of the most remarkable women I've ever known. She was a noble lady. Let me give you an example of how she worked.

"We had outgrown the three little buildings on the campus, and the Fire Department was about to condemn them anyway. Louise found a beautiful vacant lot nearby at 806 West Adams Boulevard, and she arranged for a mortgage with the Bank of America. There was a magnificent tree on the property, and one day, while we were looking at it, Louise said, 'We've got to keep that tree. We must have complete control of what we build here, without the possibility that a bank might tell us to cut the tree down.' "

"On the spot, Louise and I decided to raise our own money by sponsoring a charity baseball game at the old Wrigley Field in Los Angeles. It was spring training time for the major league teams, and through my Baltimore connections, I arranged for the Orioles to come in to play the Chicago Cubs. In the meantime, Louise set up a luncheon at the Biltmore Hotel with ten of the top business leaders in Southern California, including Walt Disney. She talked them into each guaranteeing to buy five thousand dollars worth of tickets for the game, giving us fifty thousand dollars to start with. That helped make the game a sellout, and we cleared one hundred thousand dollars. Louise paid off the mortgage, began construction, and saved the tree. The tree is still there, and the clinic is still there, and the tree is almost as famous as the clinic."

From that point on, Louise Tracy staffed the clinic with ear specialists, psychologists and specialized teachers. She expanded into satellite clinics and an international correspondence course for the parents of the deaf. She got government and university grants for the clinic's research projects. She was awarded numerous honorary degrees and served on Presidential task forces. She became as distinguished in her field as Tracy was in acting. In fact, in a speech Tracy made at the John Tracy Clinic dedication ceremonies, he said, "You honor me because I am a movie actor, a star in Hollywood terms. Well, there's nothing I've ever done that can match what Louise has done for deaf children and their parents."

This was more than idle talk from this complex man who now was living apart from his wife. He spent nearly half a million dollars of his own money in the early days when the clinic had virtually no other source of funding. He arranged for world premieres of his films to be held as charity benefit affairs for the clinic. Ex-MGM publicist Esmé Chandlee says, "Our department at the studio was always doing things for the John Tracy Clinic. If they wanted stars for fund-raising teas and such, we supplied the stars. If they wanted publicity help for their fund-raising tennis tournaments, we supplied the help. But we always had to make it look as though Tracy and his wife still were together."

Jessie Blakiston says,

"Hardly anybody in our clinic set knew that there even was a rift between Tracy and Louise. She was such a lady that you could

145

never sense it from her. She kept her home life completely separate from her clinic life. Only once a year, would she have dinner at her house for the Board of Directors. Spencer wasn't there, but everyone would take it for granted that he was away working on a film."

Mrs. Blakiston was aware of the rift because of her contacts in journalism and the movie industry, "But," she says, "all I can tell you is that he always was there when we needed him, if he was available. I can say the same about his attitude toward his children. I don't think there was a single parents' affair at Susie's Westlake school that he didn't attend, big movie star or not."

This is all the more remarkable, because, in those years, 1942 to 1946, the big movie star was not doing too well. Again, it was an outside factor which affected his career, World War II. Many of the good writers and directors were away in military service, and MGM found itself hard-pressed to come up with suitable screen properties for their off-beat superstar. Patriotic war pictures were in vogue, but they mostly called for the services of younger actors who could realistically play combat soldiers, sailors and airmen. Tracy was in his early forties, but looked older. His dark red hair was beginning to be touched with gray. His face, already lined, gave signs of his recurring ill-health (this time it was kidney and bladder problems, probably alcohol-induced, like many of his other ailments).

Tracy made only four pictures during the war years, after he had finished *Keeper of the Flame* with Hepburn. Before that, he had done *Tortilla Flat,* which, he later told Don Taylor, "was one of my worst, because I never could connect with the fishing village characters John Steinbeck wrote about." In 1943 and 1944, *A Guy Named Joe, The Seventh Cross* and *Thirty Seconds Over Tokyo* were released. They were all war pictures, and none was what you could call a Tracy blockbuster. To work him into the patriotic movie trend, MGM cast him, respectively, as the ghost of a flying ace who comes back to help his squadron, a German anti-fascist who escapes from a concentration camp, and General Jimmy Doolittle, a comparatively minor role in a film starring the young Van Johnson and the young Robert Walker. Interestingly *A Guy Named Joe* was the film in which Tracy saved Johnson's budding career by insisting that Metro hold up production until Johnson recovered from his motor accident. It also was a film in which, semi-drunk, he needled Irene Dunne to such an extent (about her clothes, her hairdo, her bustline, her slightly longish nose) that she threatened to walk out of the picture until Louis B. Mayer himself had to intercede to restore peace.

Much of Tracy's curmudgeonry and inactivity

during this period was due to the fact that Katharine Hepburn was back in New York, doing
Philip Barry's play *Without Love*. He finally be-
took himself to a suite in the Waldorf-Astoria and
remained there through much of the play's run.

MGM apparently took the hint and bought
Without Love as the studio's next Tracy-Hepburn
vehicle. Metro's Benny Thau said, "We hoped this
would quiet Spence down and that it would be a
good picture, even though it wasn't a very good
play. We got Donald Ogden Stewart to rewrite the
play."

It didn't work. The story was still mostly focused on the woman's role, as Barry originally had
conceived it. But Barry made it clear that he hated
Stewart's screen version. The movie, like the play,
was about Tracy, a Washington scientist in World
War II, who enters into a loveless marriage of
convenience with his assistant, Hepburn. But the
film varied from the stage version in wit, as
Hepburn provokes the loveless marriage into a
romantic one, with the help of two extraordinary
supporting players, Lucille Ball and Keenan Wynn.
There was more of the snappy Tracy-Hepburn
dialogue, but Kate got the good reviews, along
with Lucy and Keenan who, according to some
critics, stole the picture. James Agee wrote in *The
Nation,* "It is good to see Lucille Ball doing so
well with a kind of role new to her; and I have a
hard time breaking myself against the idea that

Keenan Wynn is the best actor in Hollywood."

Normally Tracy would bridle at such statements about another actor in a film in which *he* was the star, but he had had a lot of fun with Wynn on the set, and they became friends for life. Tracy did not resent this possibly exaggerated praise of Keenan.

But, according to Keenan, Tracy *did* begin to express a worry that maybe, once again, the acting magic was slipping away, even with Hepburn.

Chapter Fourteen

One of the most puzzling episodes in Tracy's career was his decision to return to the Broadway stage in 1945. He was a major movie star in Hollywood, a two-time Oscar winner, ranked number four at the box-office in theatre-owner polls. So why did he do it? Why expose himself again to the rigours of eight performances a week? And why risk a possible disaster, which his excursion back to the theatre turned out to be?

The easy answer, one which occurs in the Tracy mythology, is that Hepburn induced him to do it. After all, she herself returned to the stage from time to time to resharpen her acting talents and might very well have persuaded Tracy to do the same after his disappointment over *Without Love*. Also, the play was to be directed by her dear friend Garson Kanin. And the play itself, *The Rugged Path,* was written by Robert E. Sherwood, a distinguished dramatist and confidant of Franklin D. Roosevelt whom Kate greatly admired.

A different theory is advanced by Victor Samrock, business manager of The Playwrights Company which produced the play. At forty-one when America became embroiled in World War II, Tracy never served in the military, as did Clark Gable, who was only one year younger. Gable was childless and Tracy a father of two, reason enough for him not to feel guilty about it. But he did. Samrock says, "Robert Sherwood told me Tracy made three separate offers to go overseas for the USO or the Office of War Information, but each time he disappeared and never made the scheduled trip. On one occasion, he ended up in a padded cell in Chicago, suffering with the DTs after an alcoholic binge. I know about the padded cell because I was told about it by a good friend of mine who was Katharine Hepburn's manager."

According to Samrock, Tracy, as the war neared its end in the summer of 1945, contacted Sherwood, winner of three Pulitzer prizes for his plays, a White House speech-writer, and Director of Overseas Operations for the Office of War Information. Says Samrock,

"Sherwood was completing a new play, *The Rugged Path,* which was about a war journalist patterned after Ernie Pyle. Tracy wanted to do the play. Sherwood told me it was because of Tracy's terrible sense of conscience over his three missed overseas trips; that he felt that by doing this war play he would, in a way, be making up for his lack of duty in the war."

Everything started out fine at first. Samrock says, "Tracy read the completed play and liked it. He and Sherwood had a very nice relationship. We assembled a large cast, including Martha Sleeper and Jan Sterling, and got ready to begin rehearsals in a New York theater. Tracy was very pleasant to me. About twice a week throughout this entire experience with the play, he'd invite me to have dinner with him in his suite at the Waldorf-Astoria Hotel. His brother Carroll always was there; he seemed like pretty much of a stooge to me. Miss Hepburn usually was there, too. From what I remember, Hepburn didn't have too much influence on Tracy. He was a pretty tough guy with her and with everyone else. I knew her as a very marvellous star, but she acted like a schoolgirl in front of him."

Despite the socializing, there were early signs of trouble.

"I remember it very vividly," says Samrock. "I had drawn up the Tracy contract and I had given it to Sherwood to have it signed by the star. I kept saying to Sherwood, 'Where's the contract? Where's the contract?'

"Bob would reply, 'We've got to deal with Tracy. I'm not concerned.'

"But two days before we were going into rehearsal, I got a call from Carroll Tracy. He said, 'Spencer thinks the deal should be improved.'

"The Tracys now wanted a share of the profits. I said to Carroll, 'The deal had been agreed upon. Spencer might get a share of the profits in some future deal, but it's not this one.' I felt that this was some form of Hollywood blackmail which we do not practice on the New York stage.

"Carroll said, 'In that case, you have no contract.'

"To my dying day, I'll always remember this as an act of courage on the part of a playwright, who seeing his play go right down the drain, said, 'We'll call it off and recast it and do it next year.' Sherwood went to the company the next day at what was to be the first rehearsal and told them what had happened. Everybody disbanded.

"Then Tracy called Sherwood and recanted. He said, 'I'm sorry. I'm going to come to rehearsal.'" He then signed the contract on the terms which he previously had agreed.

Like all bullies, he backed down when his bluff was called. But things never were the same between him and Sherwood after that. It wasn't that Tracy didn't like the play. It gave him a chance to do a *Front Page*-type newspaperman story to which he was admirably suited. But after talking to friends, he had a change of heart and lost his zeal, as I understand he frequently did. He kept saying, 'What am I doing here? I'm a big star in Hollywood.'"

Nevertheless, rehearsals proceeded satisfactorily and the play began its out of town tryouts in Providence, then went on to Boston and Washington. The reviews were lukewarm, but there were some good ones. They were similar to what Wolcott Gibbs later wrote in *The New Yorker:* "Mr. Tracy has a winning modesty of bearing, almost as if he were uncomfortably denying some foolish charge of being an actor. It is hard to imagine what the play would have done without him." According to press reports, Tracy began demanding rewrites. He missed a couple of performances in Boston, and word got around that he was drunk and couldn't perform. "That was not true," says Samrock. "He was genuinely ill. He had a severe cold and came back in a couple of days."

The Rugged Path opened in New York at the

Plymouth Theater on 10 November 1945. Again there were mixed reviews from the critics, "but not to the extent", says Samrock, "that a little support from the star could have turned it into a hit. People wanted to see Tracy, who himself had received good reviews, but in every press conference, he kept knocking the production, saying things like, 'I don't know how long I'll be able to stay in the play. The play is no good. Sherwood should rewrite it.' Every time he did that, I, as the manager, could see an appreciable drop in the receipts at the box-office.' "

Continues Samrock: "By now, Robert Sherwood was in no mood to rewrite the play, even if it were practical to do so at that late date, which it wasn't. Bob was completely demoralized. He and Tracy had not even been speaking for months. Sherwood had had enormous hits on Broadway, including the prize winners *Idiot's Delight, There Shall Be No Night,* and *Abe Lincoln in Illinois,* and he was not used to such treatment from an actor. He felt that if Tracy didn't keep knocking the play and sabotaging it, it could have played for a year on Broadway and then gone on to make a fortune on the road, as we in The Playwrights Company did with Ingrid Bergman in *Joan of Lorraine,* another not too well received play, and with Deborah Kerr in *Tea and Sympathy.*"

Even so, *The Rugged Path* ran for eighty-one performances at the Plymouth Theater.

"Finally," says Samrock, "with Tracy continuing to say to the press that the play was no good, there wasn't enough money coming in at the box-office and we had to close down. Why did Tracy do it this way? He had a very unusual contract which gave him the option of walking out at any time just by giving us two weeks" notice. But that would have sullied his reputation. He would have been directly responsible for closing down the production. Instead, he chose the more subtle method of closing us down by invective and innuendo, making Sherwood and me the villains. Unfortunately, books on the subject still report it that way. Interestingly, the book *Tracy and Hepburn*, by the director of the play, Garson Kanin, almost completely sloughs off *The Rugged Path* and makes no mention of the controversy."

Interestingly, too, aside from the basic controversy, this peculiar episode in Tracy's life once again reveals the dichotomy of the man, the contradiction, the enigma. On the positive side, he did not drink at all during the entire run of the rehearsals and the production, according to Samrock, "although we had been led to believe that that would be a constant potential problem, a sword of Damocles hanging over our heads."

Also, Tracy performed a valiant act when the play was in its Washington tryout. A special performance was arranged at the National Theater for President Truman, his family and staff, for the Justices of the Supreme Court, members of Congress, and a group of wounded war veterans from local Veterans Administration hospitals. The problem was that the National Theater practised a policy of racial segregation in those days, and the wounded veterans were carefully screened as to race. Blacks were being excluded.

According to Garson Kanin, Tracy flew into a massive fury when he found out about this. He flatly refused to play the performance. As a result, the White House intervened with the private owners of the theatre, and, in a matter of hours, the National's segregation rules were suspended. Tracy went on as scheduled, and the veterans, black and white together, arrived on buses with their wheelchairs and crutches, and seemed to enjoy the performance.

On the other hand, the dark side of Tracy emerged in an incident involving a birthday gift for him. As Victor Samrock relates it,

"A member of the cast took up a collection for the gift, but one maverick kid, Rex Williams, refused to contribute saying, 'Nuts to that. I'm working for minimum scale and Tracy's getting thousands of dollars.' It turned out to be a mistake. Williams's recalcitrance was reported to Tracy, and, from then on, it was hell on earth for that kid. When Tracy played a scene with Williams, he'd glare at him with hatred and distaste. He'd do sly actors' tricks, like turning his head away in the middle of Williams's major lines, so that the youngster would be thrown off stride and his speech would come out garbled. After a while, Williams became so nervous that he told me he couldn't take the pressure and wanted to quit. I said, 'Don't quit, because if you can learn to handle this, the experience will stand you in good stead later on in life.'

"Looking back on the entire experience of *The Rugged Path,* I have to think that the Spencer Tracy story is a sad one indeed. I believe that his intentions were good, that there was a good man underneath. But somewhere deep inside, perhaps because of the emotional turmoil in his life, there was a bad half of him which often prevented him from carrying out the good intentions."

Chapter Fifteen

There has always been a mysterious gap in chronicles of Tracy's life—the period immediately after the closing of *The Rugged Path* on Broadway, early in 1946. This was the first year, since Tracy came to Hollywood, that he did not make a single picture. In 1942, a typical year for Tracy at MGM, he did *Woman of the Year, Tortilla Flat* and *Keeper of the Flame;* in 1947, the year *after* the mysterious gap, he made *The Sea of Grass* and *Cass Timberlane.*

So what happened in that undetailed period between *The Rugged Path* and *The Sea of Grass?*

There are some significant clues. For one thing, it is known that Tracy remained in New York after the closing of the Sherwood play. Victor Samrock says that he ran into him about six weeks after the show folded. "He was dining with Garson Kanin at Frankie and Johnny's Restaurant," says

161

Samrock, "and Tracy chatted pleasantly with me, acting as if nothing had happened between us."

Another clue is that former MGM executive Eddie Lawrence speaks vaguely about "the big drunk incident in New York," implying that it was one of Tracy's worst, and that it occurred soon after World War II.

Don Taylor, who later co-starred with Tracy in *Father of the Bride* and *Father's Little Dividend,* provides the key clue.

"It was one of the craziest things that ever happened to me," Taylor told me. "It must have been a few months after the war, probably in the Spring of 1946. It had to be. I was still in the military service and acting in the Air Force musical *Winged Victory* on Broadway, but I'd been under contract to MGM since 1942 and I'd been planning to go back to work there right after my discharge.

"It so happened that my wife at the time, Phyllis Avery, had a little gynecological problem and was a patient at Doctors Hospital on the Upper East Side of New York. Then, as now, Doctors Hospital was one of the best in the city. It was known, besides, as a luxurious place where physicians could treat celebrity patients without much danger of their privacy being invaded. I knew that a lot of big names had been hidden out there for drying out

162

from boozing."

One afternoon, Taylor had paid a visit to his wife on the obstetrical/gynecological floor, which was reserved exclusively for women patients. Taylor said,

"I came out of my wife's room and suddenly found myself surrounded in the corridor by a lot of guys I recognized from MGM in Los Angeles. The leader of the group was Whitey Hendry, the chief of security at the studio. I said, 'Whitey, what the fuck are you doing here?' Hendry just said, 'Shut up,' and tried to block my view of a trolley that was surrounded by him and his men. I already had seen who was on it. It was Spencer Tracy, and he was twisting and turning inside a strait-jacket. He was being wheeled into a room on the women's floor. At the door, Hendry turned back to me and said, 'This is very hush-hush. You didn't see *anything*. If you open your mouth and say one word about this, I'll have your ass at the studio.'

"And I have kept my mouth shut until now, forty years later. I respected Spence too much and never mentioned the incident when I worked with him later. But maybe now the world should know about Tracy's guts in fighting back from an extreme alcoholic episode like this and continuing to do such magnificent work when it was over. While she was in the hospital, my wife found out that he had been booked into a room to dry out, but that some dumb bastard had smuggled a bottle in to him on a visit. Tracy had drunk the bottle and went into delirium tremens. They got the DTs under control but notified the studio, which sent Hendry out with his men. Tracy was put on the women's floor because nobody could possibly find him there."

The Doctors Hospital incident illustrates many things. Tracy did not drink during the run of *The Rugged Path,* and seemed fine when Samrock saw him again in New York six weeks later. What set him off? Was it delayed guilt about his part in the failure of the play? Was it lack of self-esteem and anxiety over the fact that he had been in another failure (Don Taylor says that he talked about being similarly degraded by having been in a bad picture, *Tortilla Flat,* four years before). Was he torn by his love for Hepburn, who was with him in New York, and suffering remorse over not being in close contact with his children and his wife, Louise, who was now having great success with the establishment of her John Tracy Clinic in Los Angeles? Who knows what sets an alcoholic off and precipitates a "slip"? Probably only Katharine

Hepburn knows, in Tracy's case, and she will not talk about it.

Another thing which the Doctors Hospital incident points up is the sophisticated logistic system set up by Metro Goldwyn Mayer to protect the illusion that none of its great galaxy of stars ever did anything to offend public morals. In those days, autocrats like Louis B. Mayer felt the public should be protected from the stars' fallibility. There may have been some validity to this line of thinking. The movie stars of the 1930s and 1940s were America's royalty, and no country wants its royalty to be sullied. It should be remembered that Mayer was instrumental in hiring Louella Parsons and, later, Hedda Hopper, to ensure that in their columns at least, the conventions would not be flouted. It worked, for a time, until both Miss Parsons and Miss Hopper grew restive under the system.

But Mayer had more effective and more direct anti-sullying techniques, proof of which is that, to this day, people are generally unaware of Tracy's peccadilloes.

The resident genius of Louis B. Mayer's star-protection system was the late Howard Strickling, the Vice President in charge of publicity at MGM. Strickling told me a good deal about how his system worked. He said it was not dissimilar from then-current systems at other studios, but that "even I, if I had been at Warner Brothers, couldn't have done much with a chronic hell-raiser and drunk like Errol Flynn." He added, "In the early days, we had guys who were just as bad — Wallace Beery and John Gilbert — but I'd tell my people, 'Remember, they may be sons-of-bitches, but like Mr. Mayer says, never forget they're our sons-of-bitches.' So my people worked doubly hard to keep their hell-raising out of the newspapers."

The keystone of Strickling's system was Whitey Hendry. "Mr. Mayer," Strickling told me,

"decided we needed a top cop who knew other top cops in the area and all over the United States, so he offered Whitey a lot of money to come with us from his job as Chief of Police of Culver City. It turned out to be a smart move. If Tracy, for example, was picked up for wrecking a hotel room in Beverly Hills, Whitey would call the police chief in Beverly Hills and Tracy wouldn't be booked. The studio would quietly pay for the damage he caused."

Strickling gave me another specific example:

"One night, Clark Gable got very drunk and tried to drive through, rather than around, one of the Bristol Circles in Brentwood. There are a lot of trees in the center of the Bristol Circles and Gable didn't penetrate very far. He smashed up his car and himself. The police on the scene called the captain at the West Los Angeles Division, who called Chief Parker at LA police headquarters downtown. The accident scene was roped off from the public, Gable was hustled away to a private hospital, and the incident never was reported in the police blotters—or in the press.

"For multi-problem people like Tracy, we devised an even more elaborate technique. We kept an official-looking ambulance on call at the studio. Every bar owner and hotel manager in the area knew what to do if Tracy showed up drunk and began causing a problem. They'd phone me, and I'd phone Whitey, and the ambulance would take off with a couple of our security men dressed as paramedics. They'd go to the scene, strap Tracy to a stretcher, and then rush him away in the ambulance before too many people could recognize Tracy as the trouble-maker. Considering his habit of drinking only in private, we mostly found him alone off in a room somewhere."

And then there was the general willingness of the press in those days to aid in the cover-ups. Strickling bragged to me that he knew every journalist in town and that there was not a city desk he could not call to get a story killed.

Strangely, the Strickling syndrome still exists among many of the people who worked for him in his MGM publicity department in those raucous days. They are now mostly old and retired and far removed from the studio pressures, yet they say, "I still don't think it's right to talk about *our* stars."

You say, "But the man is dead and gone for twenty years now. Just tell me the good things you remember about him."

They develop a glazed look and insist, "But I didn't really see him that much. I didn't really know him." (This, from one woman in particular, who was on the set with Tracy every day for at least ten years, and who visited him frequently in his home.)

Comments Dana Andrews, a confessed recovering alcoholic and a distinguished member of the National Council on Alcoholism,

"How sad. The cover-ups were good for the studios, but not for those of us actors who needed help. It's wrong to deny Tracy's problem to this day. It's wrong the way it always has been swept under the rug, and the way people would say, 'Oh, he was just a fun-loving, hard-drinking Irishman.' None of this aids the cause of the treatment of this disease—by recognizing it, admitting it, and seeking help.

"I personally had to make up my mind

whether I was going to go on being an actor, or be an alcoholic and not live very long."

Esmé Chandlee, one of the few ex-MGM publicists to talk, adds, "Tracy would not have lived very long—in fact, he would have died many years before he did—had it not been for Hepburn."

Chapter Sixteen

There is evidence that Tracy's heaviest drinking slackened off in the late 1940s, although there was still an occasional prodigious "slip" yet to come. Don Taylor says, "He seemed to have given up the bottle when we did *Father of the Bride* in 1950. He had been to Boston for a little surgery; he told me, 'My plumbing has deteriorated'; and he brought his doctor from Boston to visit him when we were on the set."

Taylor theorizes that this Boston physician was acquired by Tracy through the influence of Katharine Hepburn. Says Taylor,

"Spence was beginning to worry about the state of his health, the ravages of all those years of boozing, but without Hepburn it is doubtful to me that he would have done anything about it. Besides, she gave him constant strength to fight off his urges to drink. These days, when I want to say, 'Good luck to you, Spence, wherever you are,' I don't know whether to look up or down. He's probably somewhere in betwixt, but only because of Kate."

The Hepburn influence was a profound one, according to all those friends who knew them well. Chief among them was George Cukor, who directed Tracy and Hepburn in some of their greatest films *(Keeper of the Flame, Adam's Rib, Pat and Mike)*. In his latter years, Tracy lived in a little rented house on Cukor's property at St. Ives Place, on the border of Beverly Hills, and Hepburn was frequently there with him. "The bedroom of this little house," said Cukor, "was almost like a monk's cell when Spencer lived there. It had an oak chest, one chair, a bed, and that's all. It had the air of a place where a man might do penance." Often, however, Tracy and Hepburn were guests in the magnificent salon of Cukor's own mansion, a couple of hundred feet away. Cukor was friendlier with them than anyone.

I interviewed Cukor for the *New York Times* in 1978, and, although my story was about *The Corn is Green* which he was directing on television with Miss Hepburn as his star, much of our conversation drifted off to his recollection of the Hepburn-Tracy relationship.

"There was something exceptionally sweet about it," said Cukor. "Though they were both extremely sophisticated people, he was like a little boy with her and she was like a little girl with him. He could be extremely gruff with her, that was the little roughneck boy from Milwaukee filtering through, but he had enormous respect for her and he *listened* to her.

"In the terrible matter of his drinking, I believe she *did* extend his life. She made sure he went to the finest doctors when the inevitable complications of his drinking set in, and she even went so far as to tie him to his bed in the little house when she sensed the symptoms indicating that one of his major disappearance-binges was coming on. Mostly she helped him by distracting him from his drinking with love, and with finding fascinating things they could do together in the entire new world of culture she had opened up to him.

"They went to museums together, they made several trips to Europe together, she introduced him to great music and literature. It was fun watching them wandering around my property hand in hand, looking at the flowers, and then sitting down in the sun to read, or to listen to a Brahms concerto or a symphony on their portable record-player. Some of the rough edges already had worn off Tracy with his interest in art and his own painting, and he already had some distinguished friends. For example, somehow he had got to know Supreme Court Justice William O. Douglas, who adored him. But with Kate, he soon was able to discuss Shakespeare and D. H. Lawrence in my salon, and he moved into the Hollywood intellectual set, which included Noël Coward, David Niven and Laurence Olivier. Strange, because he also still kept seeing his old buddies, like Pat O'Brien and Jimmy Cagney, which was a new experience for Kate.

"They stayed in Kate's houses in town, at the beach, and in New York and Connecticut. They always were very discreet about maintaining their privacy. They never went out to eat in a public restaurant. Once, when they took a vacation at The Racquet Club in Palm Springs, they had an apartment converted for them in the old servants quarters, and no one ever saw them.

"What I remember most is that they could bicker and argue and say dreadful things to one another, but always come out of it laughing and hugging, like teenagers. As far as benefits are concerned, it was not a one-sided affair. I've known Kate since 1933 when she was a little girl and I was directing her in *Little Women.* There was an enormous change in her after she worked with Spencer in *Woman of the Year* and fell in love with him. She's a strong, dominant woman, who was considered cold, with no sex appeal. Little by little, she could have become a typical old maid. However, her relationship with extrovert, down-to-earth Tracy and the sexual attraction she admits to, was good for her. Without his influence, for example, it's unlikely that she could have given one of the great screen performances of all time with Humphrey Bogart in *The African Queen.*

"I always took delight in the conversation between Spence and Kate. It always was male-female sparring, much like the dialogue in *Pat and Mike.* I remember once when Kate was talking about the pleasures of nesting: 'I like nothing better than to buy a house and then fill it with all the things I cherish, buy all those silly wonderful things that make a house a heartwarming experience to return to.'

" 'Not me,' said Spence, 'I don't want to own anything that I can't pack in the baggage car of a train to Chicago.'

"Another time, Kate was talking about the wonderful liberal tradition of her parents back East in Connecticut. 'Oh, sure,' teased

Spence, 'I'll never forget when we sat with your father, the doctor, in that sea-side place at Saybrook and he was carrying on about Henry Wallace, and how everybody else was jumping on the rights of the common man. Just then, a common man set foot on the property to get to the beach, and your father stopped in the middle of his argument to get up and holler at the man to get the hell off his land.'

"Kate didn't take offense. She just broke up laughing."

Gene Kelly has a slightly different perspective of the Tracy-Hepburn relationship in the 1950s.

"I always had a lot of people dropping by my house in those days," says Kelly. "There were no invitations. People would just come and we'd talk politics and we'd play a lot of word games, charades, twenty questions, Jotto, and such. The funny thing about Spence, is that he'd just sit there quietly and sip a coke. I never saw him take a drink. Katie was more attuned to the people at these little evenings. They were Adolph Green, Betty Comden, Oscar Levant, Fredric March, every musician and composer who happened to be in town. We all were of the liberal bent, big admirers of Franklin D. Roosevelt, the New Deal, the

Fair Deal. Politically, we all were the opposite of Spence. Katie joined in the political discussions, but everybody had too much respect for Spence's feelings and nobody talked politics to him. Also, we knew he didn't like the word games, so we didn't play them when he was there.

"My wife, Betsy Blair, was a good friend of George Cukor's, and we would be invited up for George's famous soirées, with all the great ladies he knew, Ethel Barrymore, Fanny Brice, Katie Hepburn. Funny, but Spence, who lived just down the hill, never showed up, when I was there, at least. Also, we Irishmen in town always had a big St. Patrick's Day party every year, frequently at my house. Pat O'Brien and Pat Harrington would sing Irish songs and we'd all have a wonderful time. Spence, who was very proud of being Irish, never showed up at these shindigs, either alone or with Katie. I could never figure that out.

"When Katie was away, my wife, Betsy, always seemed to know that Spence might be in his little house with nothing to do. I suspect George Cukor used to tip her off. In any event, we'd invite him to our place, and he'd come, and sit quietly and sip his coke. He'd chat amiably enough, and we stayed away from the politics and the word games, and after about two hours he'd leave. He sure was a sad lonely guy when Katie wasn't there."

And so, once again, we have two conflicting views of Tracy. There was the Tracy who animatedly discussed art and literature with Cukor, Noël Coward, Laurence Olivier and Hepburn. And then there was the Tracy who sat quietly with Gene Kelly, Oscar Levant, Fredric March and Hepburn, and veered away from politics and word games. Also, there was the once staunchly Irish Catholic Tracy who spent every Thursday night in the 1930s with the Cagneys, O'Briens and McHughs, but who now was uninterested in any overt show of Hibernianism, even though, as Gene Kelly suggested, "Katie would have loved it."

Chapter Seventeen

Tracy aged more quickly than most actors, and by the time he was fifty, he was mostly playing father, or elder statesman roles. He was even a grandpa in *Father's Little Dividend*. The exceptions were when Garson Kanin and Ruth Gordon came up with another of their delicious Hepburn-Tracy scripts, like *Adam's Rib* and *Pat and Mike,* and he was playing that grumpy, needling, mature romantic again. It didn't seem to matter what he was playing. Even in the movie depression caused by McCarthyism, the Hollywood Blacklist, and the advent of television, Tracy films, good or bad, kept making money. He renegotiated his contract with MGM and now was required to make only one film a year.

The early 1950s were both good and bad times for Tracy. He exulted when his wife, Louise, won her own Woman of the Year award; and when their son, John, having totally overcome his hearing impairment and now lip-reading and speaking perfectly, graduated from school, got a job as an artist at the Disney Studios, and married. Tracy became a grandfather for real in 1955 when Joseph Spencer Tracy was born.

In his strange double life (he said he could not contemplate divorce because of his staunch Catholicism), Tracy spent many months touring Europe with Kate Hepburn, as incognito as possible. Their favourite places were London, where they spent a lot of time with Laurence Olivier and David Niven, Amsterdam and Paris, where they happily toured the museums and art galleries.

On the other hand, Tracy went into depressions and reverted to his alcoholic disappearances when Hepburn was away, for example when she made *The African Queen.*

When John's wife, Nadine, divorced him and got custody of two-year-old Joseph Spencer, Tracy also cut loose.

But, as usual, Tracy bounced back from such reverses, and settled down to make one of the toughest, and one of the best films of his career. It was a difficult project for everyone concerned, and typical of Tracy's dealings with MGM throughout his career.

Millard Kaufman, the distinguished writer of the screenplay, filled me in on the details of the making of *Bad Day at Black Rock,* from its early, inauspicious, beginnings.

Said Kaufman:

"I was working at Metro in 1953, when Dore Schary, the head of production, called me in. He said the studio was having a lot of trouble finding a film property for Tracy to star in. The year was nearly up in Tracy's contract and they just *had* to come up with something in a hurry and get his acquiescence. Dore showed me a short story they had bought. It was called "Bad Day at Hondo." I read it and said it was terrible. Dore agreed. He then asked me to read a screenplay based on the short story. I said, 'It's terrible, too.' Once again he agreed and wondered if I'd be interested in rewriting the script so that it would be palatable to Tracy and also be a good picture. I said I'd try."

Next, there came a meeting with Tracy, Schary, Kaufman and Herman Hoffman, who was to be the associate producer. Kaufman said,

"Dore had an unbelievable belief in himself and his ability to sell. At the meeting, he just winged the essentials of the plot to Tracy who, in his usual manner, didn't say anything. He gave Spence just the short story to read, not even mentioning the screenplay that we all thought was so bad. The result was predictable. A few days later Schary told me that Spence had called him and said, 'How dare you give me this kind of shit. I'm supposed to be the best male actor in America, and you can jam this up your ass.' "

Nevertheless, Schary gave Kaufman the go-ahead to proceed with the script. The writer skilfully refined the story of the World War II officer who has just returned from the service, and journeys to a crossroads hamlet, just "an inhabited place" in the California desert, to present a posthumous medal, won by one of his soldiers, to the boy's Japanese father. After unrelieved hostility and peril at the hands of the men of the town, the officer finally deduces that they have murdered the Japanese father. The offbeat story was filled with suspense, foreboding and displays of the officer's courage and determination.

MGM loved Kaufman's new script. Schary was now determined to get Tracy back into the film. Kaufman recalls,

"First, Dore said to me, 'Let's make him a guy with only one usable arm. I never knew an actor who could resist playing a cripple.' I said I thought that was a good idea, and then Dore proceeded with his next step. He was very good at this sort of manipulation and he seemed to know all the tricks to get at Spence's vulnerabilities. He had submitted my script to Alan Ladd, who wasn't even in town, and had gotten a 'no' from Ladd's agent. But Dore took the script and sent it by messenger to Tracy with a cover note saying, 'Alan Ladd has agreed to do the picture, but you are still my first choice, and I thought you might be interested in reading the script.' Two hours later, Tracy called back and told Schary, 'I want to do the picture. The hell with Alan Ladd.' "

Such were the devious ways of Hollywood, then and now.

But there were still many hurdles on the path to actual production. The director, Richard Brooks, was dropped and replaced with one of Tracy's favourites, John Sturges. The producer, Charles Schnee, was dropped, and Schary himself decided to produce the film. Tracy was sent to MGM's wardrobe department to be fitted with the one suit he was to wear throughout the picture, but he vetoed everything they showed him on the grounds that none of the suits was grungy enough. Says Kaufman, "Spence told me, 'Where would a guy just out of the Army, and with no money, go to buy his first civilian suit?' It was a manifestation of his perfectionism as an actor. So he went downtown in Los Angeles to a discount clothing store and came back with two identical cheap-looking suits that were just right for the part." This undoubtedly did not make Metro's wardrobe department happy, but it was never Tracy's custom to promote glee among subsidiary studio departments, such as wardrobe and make-up (make-up artists were his particular anathema and he no longer would allow them to come within ten feet of him).

According to Kaufman, another flap preceded the commencement of production. He says, "Our picture still was called 'Bad Day at Hondo', when, to everyone's surprise, there came the release of a John Wayne movie called *Hondo*. So our title went out the window." Such coincidental flaps can cause weeks of delays at a studio, while everyone tries to think of a new title. In this case, Kaufman was out in Arizona, with Arthur Loew Jr., looking for locations for another picture, when they stopped for gas at one of the bleakest places either of them had ever seen. It was not even a "wide place in the road," just a gas station and a post office. Kaufman looked at the identifying sign on the post office. The name was Black Rock, Arizona. Kaufman rushed to the phone and called the studio. "I've got the title for the Tracy picture," he said. "We'll call it 'Bad Day at Black Rock', but we'll still shoot it in California."

That problem having been solved, there were just a few other minor contretemps before the start of production. Kaufman had written into the script a gimmick, whereby Tracy's one-armed character, Macreedy, had developed the technique of lighting a match with his thumb nail. Kaufman says,

"Spence came to me and said, 'Let's face it. I'm not as young as I used to be and my hands can't do what they did twenty years ago. Besides, every son-of-abitch I ever heard of who came out of the Army, the Navy or the Marine Corps, always had one of those goddam Zippo lighters.' So Zippo it was, even though I'd spent a lot of time developing the thumbnail match-lighting trick for dramatic effect in a lot of scenes."

Production began on the MGM lot, and, according to Kaufman, most of the picture was filmed there, with only a few days on location, at a miserable spot, in the heat of summer, on the edge of Death Valley. Much has been made of the hardships of this location, allegedly impelling Tracy to go off on weekend drinking benders, but Kaufman says this simply is not true. "Spence was there only briefly," says Kaufman, "mostly shooting exterior shots, and entrances and exits at replicas of buildings we had constructed on the set back at Metro. It was not very taxing for him. I knew all about his reputation for boozing, but I never saw him drunk on this picture." Others report that, while the rest of the cast guzzled a lot of beer to cool off in the oppressive heat, Tracy spent most of his off-hours in his air-conditioned trailer, reading and sipping iced coffee.

Kaufman says,

"It was a helluva cast, Robert Ryan, Anne Francis, Ernie Borgnine, Dean Jagger, Walter Brennan, Lee Marvin, but Spence seemed to socialize on the set with only one of them. That was Robert Ryan, a fellow Irishman. Spence had great respect for Bob as an actor. One day he said to me, 'Bob is so good in this part, he scares the hell out of me. Does he scare the hell out of you as a bad guy?' I said yes and he said, 'That's good. It means he'll scare the hell out of the audience, too.'

"Spence was more knowledgeable about film than anyone I've ever known. He was enormously aware of what he could or could not do. He knew all the technical aspects of movie-making. Richard Burton once told me he didn't know a thing about film until he met Elizabeth Taylor. He said Elizabeth taught him that the stage is a medium of action, whereas film is a medium of reaction. Spence knew this. He was better at responding and reacting than anyone I've ever seen work. Also, he carried his personal mannerisms into his acting, and they were very effective. For example, he always scratched his nose when he was thinking in real life. He did that, too, when he was acting. I also noticed that he pushed his tongue out of the corner of his mouth when he was sceptical or cynical about something. How many times have you seen him do this on film, conveying the attitude of wry incredulity without saying a word? Gable understood this business of reacting, too. He once told a director, 'I don't care what the hell scene you put me in. You don't have to give me one line, or two lines, or not even one word of dialogue. All I want is the last line and the exit.' No wonder he and Spence were so good together. They both conveyed their inner thoughts with reactions, which are hard as hell to write into a script."

Kaufman recalls that there was one incident in *Bad Day at Black Rock* in which both the brilliant and obstreperous Tracy emerged. Says Kaufman;

"It was the key scene in the picture. It was outside the Black Rock gas station, and Tracy was trying to find out from Bob Ryan what had happened to the Japanese farmer. Ryan, of course, doesn't want to tell him and keeps talking all around the subject. The scene was so difficult that we scheduled an entire day to shoot it. Tracy was so good, however, and Ryan followed along so effectively, that we finished the entire scene in one hour, from eight in the morning until nine. John Sturges, the director, just shook his head in amazement and said, 'OK, that's a take. Print it.'

"Then John got ready to move on to other scenes, which was necessary in the tight MGM schedule we faced. Spence said, 'Oh, no. This scene we just did was scheduled for a day and we've done a day's work.' To Ryan, he said, 'Bob, let's take off.' And he and Ryan stalked off the set. This left Sturges in a hole. In no way would Metro let him waste the rest of the day, so he had to shoot around Spence, which was difficult for him to do because Tracy was in nearly every scene."

On the whole, though, *Bad Day at Black Rock* was indicative of how efficient and co-operative Tracy could be under certain conditions. He liked the producer, Schary; he had great respect for the director, Sturges; he appreciated the talent of the other actors, and, as in one of his earlier triumphs, *Fury,* he seemed to feel a great sense of involvement in an expose of deep-seated intolerance among human beings.

A year later, novelist John O'Hara wrote, that *"Bad Day at Black Rock* was one of the finest motion pictures ever made. In recommending Oscars for Tracy and all the others in the production, O'Hara said:

"You are a victim of suspense, and you are an easy victim because you feel yourself not to be a person in an audience, but a spectator in the action at Black Rock. You feel the heat and aridity of the desert; you want to know what shameful thing is eating the inhabitants of this town. And above all you want to know what's going to happen. What does this man Macreedy want? What are the people hiding? . . . Maybe [this picture] will convince the Hollywood junk dealers that the good ones pay off, too."

The film earned Oscar nominations for Tracy (his fifth) and also for writer Kaufman.

Tracy, of course, didn't know that for some months, not even waiting around to see a final cut of the film (a practice not uncommon for him). The usual insecurities set in and he fled to Italy, where David Lean was making *Summertime,* with Katharine Hepburn as his star. He spent the summer with Kate and talked about possibly buying a villa in Florence and settling down there.

But MGM already had his next year's film in pre-production and he brooded about it.

With good reason, as it turned out.

Chapter Eighteen

Another view of Tracy in *Bad Day at Black Rock,* a rare and unexpected memoir, comes from Ernest Borgnine who, when he was cast as one of the most ominous villains in the film, had only been making movies for three years. He had broken through as a major actor playing the terrifying military-prison boss, Fatso, in *From Here to Eternity,* but Tracy was Mr. Tracy to him then; and Borgnine still referred to him, not as Spence or Spencer, but always as Mr. Tracy when he spoke to me about *Bad Day at Black Rock* more than thirty years later.

Said Borgnine:

"You could say that when I worked with Mr. Tracy in the picture, I was in awe of him. But it was more than that. You know, to me, he was the world's greatest actor, and my

God, here I am working with the man.

"The first time that I ever saw Mr. Tracy was at a distance. I say at a distance because he and the director, John Sturges, were always off to one side. Then John said, 'All right, we're going to do the scene where Macreedy arrives back in the hotel in his jeep,' which was right after the scene—which we hadn't done yet—where I knocked him down that hill. It was our first scene together, and you know, my God, how was I going to handle it when I thought of his previous reputation?

"Anyway, he came toward me, and as he came toward me, I blanked out. I forgot every line I ever knew in my life. Then *he* blanked out in my mind, too. All I could see coming toward me, all I could see were the two Academy Awards he had won, you know. I said to myself, 'My God, waddaya gonna do, waddaya gonna do?' But suddenly, as Mr. Tracy came up, my first line came back to me: 'Well, if it ain't Macreedy, the All American road hog' and we went through the whole bloody scene. One take. Bam, bam, bam. Walter Brennan, who was watching, gave me the thumbs up sign, and then Mr. Tracy came back through the door where the scene ended. Mr. Tracy took my hand, and he shook it, and he said, 'Hey, you're OK. That's the way I like to do a scene. Thank you very much.

We'll be talking.' Wow! I was kinda like in a daze."

(Keep in mind that this was not a star-struck young neophyte talking. Borgnine was *already* recognized as a premier movie performer, with eight films in addition to *From Here to Eternity,* and a stage success on Broadway in *Harvey.* He soon would even be considered for one of the same roles that Tracy himself played. But his awe for Tracy continued throughout the filming of *Bad Day at Black Rock.*)

Borgnine told me:

"On that set, it was pretty much a case of my watching and studying Mr. Tracy. I never saw such technique. Fr'instance, I'll never forget that long scene he did with Robert Ryan outside the gas station, the one they were gonna take a whole day to do but they finished up with it in an hour. I said to myself, 'How can an actor hide himself from the audience, just bending over and looking up occasionally? I could see that Ryan was trying to do everything but drop his pants. But there was Mr. Tracy, this man was talking to the *ground,* for Christ's sake, and only once in a while would he look up. I never saw anybody do that, just talking to the ground, and everyone's attention was riveted on *him*. It was just right for the character of Macreedy and Mr. Tracy thought up that way of doing it. The director, the great old actors like Walter Brennan and Dean Jagger, all the rest of us, we all just applauded when the scene was over."

Borgnine prides himself with coming up with a gimmick of his own, principally because it pleased Tracy. One of the key scenes of the picture was a fight between the one-armed Macreedy and the bully, Coley Trimble, played by Borgnine. It turned out to be one of the great fight scenes in movie history, to that date.

Before the scene was scheduled to be shot, Borgnine spoke with director Sturges. "I said to him," says Borgnine, "how can a man with one arm throw punches? I said, you know, it's impossible. I'd be all over him. I'd wrap him up in my arms and everything else.

"John said, 'Well, waddaya suggest?'

"I said, 'He uses Judo.'

"John said 'That's a helluva idea.'

"And that's the way we did it."

The scene had to be done with a stuntman double because of Tracy's age and infirmities, but, according to Borgnine,

Mr. Tracy sat on the side with Dore Schary, watching everything, and I could hear everything he said like he was at ringside in Madison Square Garden. Like I had a sponge in my hand filled with red dye, and when I went down once from a knee in my face, I squooshed the dye all over my face, and I could hear Mr. Tracy say, 'My God, they've killed him.' But I got up and we went right on fighting, never stopped.

"At the end, I was supposed to crash through a door. In rehearsal, the door was left just on the latch. But when we did the scene, I hit the door going about ninety-six miles an hour and some son-of-a-bitch had locked the door. I found out later who it was, it was John Sturges. But goddam, I hit the door and took the door and all with me, you know. I lay there for a minute and I said, 'Holy Christ, what happened?' And then I picked myself up slowly, came back and threw the last punch before I went down for good. Well, I tell you, Mr. Tracy came up and turned me over and he shook my hand. He said, 'What a helluva scene.' He was just thrilled to death, and I was just thrilled to death at what he said, and everybody was just applauding like crazy."

So much for a unique inside view of rough-and-tumble movie making in the days before karate and kung-fu became a staple.

195

Perhaps the most interesting incident in the Tracy-Borgnine relationship on *Bad Day at Black Rock* came a little later. Here's how Borgnine tells it:

"One day I got a call to go see Delbert Mann about a part in another picture, and Dore Schary gave me the afternoon off. Mr. Tracy says to me, 'Hey, where the hell are you going?'

"I said, 'Well, sir,' I said, 'they allowed me to go because I'm gonna read for a picture.'

"Mr. Tracy said, 'Waddaya mean, read? You don't *read* any more. Christ, you're a star.'

"I said, 'Well, that's all right for you to say, but I still gotta read for these people, otherwise I don't get the part.'

"And he said, 'Well, what's the picture about?' and I told him, and he said, 'Well OK, go ahead. You're gonna get the part. Don't worry about it. You'll be good.'

"The next morning I came back and Mr. Tracy said, 'Well?' And I said, 'Yes, *sir*, I got the part.'

"And he was thrilled, he was delighted. He was that kind of person, a wonderfully shy kind of guy that never did say too much, but God, you could see him watching and thinking, and he knew exactly what was going on all the time."

* * *

Did Tracy really know what was going on? It's doubtful, because the incident evolved into one of the great ironies of his career. The picture Borgnine left the set to read for was *Marty*. In the 1955 Oscar race, Tracy was nominated for *Bad Day at Black Rock* and was the odds on favourite for the Best Actor award. Borgnine, a dark horse, was nominated for *Marty*. Borgnine won.

But Borgnine relates still another sequel to this story. He says,

"After the Oscars, Mr. Tracy was out of the country and when he came back I went to see him over at his studio and he was in his trailer. I said, 'I just stopped by to say hello.'

"He said, 'Hello. Goddamit, I sent you a telegram of congratulations and I never got an answer back.'

"I didn't know what to say to that, and then Kate Hepburn came to my rescue.

"Kate, she was in the back of the trailer, and she stuck her head out, and she said to Mr. Tracy. '*He* won the Oscar, not you, you dummy.'

"We laughed over that. But he congratulated me, and that was the last time I ever saw him, God bless him. But I still watched everything he ever did, even the old movies on TV. You learn so much from him. God, he was a *master*. What a *master!*"

Chapter Nineteen

James Stewart will never forget a picture called *Malaya* which he made with Tracy in 1949.

"It was a constantly edgy situation," says Stewart. "Spence was more cantankerous than usual because the film was a real potboiler about two guys trying to steal rubber from under the eyes of the Japanese in South-east Asia during World War II. We knew that was a dangerous situation for Spence. He could walk out and pull one of his famous disappearances at any time. So I decided on a strategy to keep him interested in something other than the picture."

Stewart's strategy was laboriously to plan a trip to Europe and Asia which they would take together after the filming was completed. Says Stewart,

"Every day, we'd talk about what countries we were going to visit, and I kept collecting brochures to show to him. He'd pore over the brochures and talk with great excitement about Greece and Rome and the Taj Mahal. Wal, anyway, the strategy seemed to work and Spence showed up every day and did his usual fine job. When it was over, I said to him, 'Wal, have you gotten your passport yet?'

"He said, 'What passport?'

" 'For our trip to Europe and Asia,' I said.

" 'Europe and Asia?' he said, 'Why, I wouldn't go across the *street* with you, you son-of-a-bitch.' "

The Stewart film was typical of what was beginning to bug Tracy as he neared his twentieth year at MGM. Just as he had at Fox, he had become restive at the quality of films being offered to him. He had been exhilarated, or course, doing *Pat and Mike* with Hepburn in 1952. And after that shaky beginning, *Bad Day at Black Rock* had turned out to be a picture that greatly excited him.

On the whole, though, he fought with the studio about being cast in such lesser movies as *Plymouth Adventure* and *Broken Lance*. He could no longer play the romantic leading man; his hair was white, his girth was increasing. Yet he continued to be a superstar, bringing in millions for MGM at the box-office, even with the potboilers. Reorganizations on the executive levels at the studio had weakened Louis B. Mayer's power and brought Dore Schary to the fore. But that did not seem to trouble Tracy too much. "I just fought with Schary now," he once said, "instead of old L.B."

In fact, he and Schary liked one another. Schary says,

"I first got to know Spence when I was a very young assistant stage manager for his Broadway play, *The Last Mile,* in 1930. He barely was aware of *me,* of course, but later in life, one of his favorite jokes was, 'I used to look at that kid and say that he was going to grow up to be Dore Schary, head of production at Metro Goldwyn Mayer.' In 1938, Spence was in the hospital, recovering from one of his bad bouts with alcohol, and when he told the studio he wanted to get right back to work, the only script available was one I had written, *Boys Town,* which Metro previously had turned down.

"Spence got an Oscar for *Boys Town* and I got one for the original story. We then did *Edison the Man* together and I came to know him quite well. I learned about his quirks, especially his terrible insecurities about the pictures he did. Invariably he'd like a script and decide to do a picture; then he'd change his mind and say he absolutely wouldn't do it; and finally, usually just a few days before a film was ready to go, he'd reluctantly say, 'OK, I'll do it.' That's why he and I were able to get along when I was in charge of production in those troubled days—for him and for me—in the early 1950s at Metro. We reached our highpoint together with *Bad Day at Black Rock.*"

Then came a picture called *Tribute to a Bad Man,* which you will *not* find in any listings of Tracy's seventy-odd films.

The director of *Tribute to a Bad Man* was Robert Wise, who already had done *The Day the Earth Stood Still* and *Executive Suite* and who later was to direct such blockbusters as *The Sound of Music* and *West Side Story.* In 1985, he became President of the Academy of Motion Picture Arts and Sciences.

Relates Wise:

"When Metro assigned me to direct *Tribute to a Bad Man,* I was delighted to learn that Spencer Tracy was going to be my star. I had always admired his fantastic acting talents and I was looking forward to an illuminating experience. It was illuminating all right, but not in any way that I could have imagined.

"I first met Tracy when I was called into the office of Sam Zimbalist, the film's producer, to discuss Michael Blankfort's script, and Zimbalist said it would be a good idea for Tracy and me to meet and discuss the project. So Spence came in and we had a very pleasant chat. He was very enthusiastic about the script and he seemed pleased about costarring with Irene Papas, the Greek actress, whose previous work he knew about. Mostly he wanted to talk about the location I would select. He said, 'Let's find some place that hasn't been used before. I'm tired of seeing the same old locations over and over again in Westerns. We should find a spot that's way up high in the Rockies and it should have nice green fields and meadows because, after all, this is a picture about a guy who breaks and trains horses for Wells Fargo.' I agreed that our location would be green and that the best place would be at high altitude. 'Yeah, high,' he said, and we parted with Tracy again expressing his great enthusiasm for the picture. He was leaving for New York that night.

"The very next morning, he woke me up with a phone call from New York. He said, 'Bobby, do you think we're doing the right thing? Do you think this picture has a chance? Do you think it's any good?' I was amazed because just the day before he had practically been selling *me* on the film, he was so excited about it. But then I remembered what Benny Thau, a top executive at Metro had told me, that there hadn't been a picture in all the time Thau had been at the studio, when Tracy hadn't called *him* about two weeks before shooting and said, 'I can't do it. It's no good.' So I reassured Tracy and calmed him down. To this day, I don't know what was inside the man to make him so nervous and upset about all his projects."

Wise got the finished script and scouted the West for the high-altitude location Tracy said he wanted. He finally found it in the Rockies near Montrose, Colorado, about 268 miles south-west of Denver. It was a breathtakingly beautiful spot, green mountain meadow ringed by towering snow-capped peaks. Spending hundreds of thousands of dollars, the studio built an entire authentic 1870s horse-ranch on the location. It was an elaborate set, nine buildings in all, and it took the construction crews three months to complete the job.

To keep an eye on Tracy, Howard Strickling assigned one of his best publicists, Jim Merrick, as the on the site "unit man" for the production. Merrick became the chief chronicler of the strange saga of *Tribute to a Bad Man*.

Merrick told me,

.

"During the months of construction of the set at Montrose, Tracy was brooding around the studio. But the first inkling I had that something was bugging Tracy about *Tribute to a Bad Man* was when he stopped me on the lot at Metro and asked, 'Who is this broad, Irene Papas?' I told him she had done some fine film work in Greece with top directors like Michael Cacoyannis. He asked me about her height, and when I told him Irene was a big rawboned five feet ten inches, he just said 'Hmm', and turned away. That didn't bother me because I remembered how he had worried about Hepburn's height when they first met on *Woman of the Year.*"

The next incident, however, *did* cause Merrick some concern. He said, "Production was scheduled to begin in June, and, at first, Tracy asked permission to come to the location early, in order to accustom himself to the eight thousand foot altitude. He never showed up. Then the cast and crew arrived. Still no Tracy. The director, Bobby Wise, began to shoot without him."

Says Wise, "I was able to do that because there were a lot of scenes involving Irene Papas and young Robert Francis, who also was in the cast. I did everything I could with the Papas and Francis scenes which did not include Tracy."

Continued publicist Merrick,

"On Friday evening, five days after shooting began, Tracy finally arrived in Montrose. He drove up in a Thunderbird with the trunk loaded with murder mysteries. The next morning at 11 a.m. I drove him out to the location, about forty-five minutes away. He looked at the ranch buildings with the beautiful backdrop of the snow-capped Rockies and said it was great. Then he went around shaking hands with all the technicians he knew in the crew. It was lunchtime and he sat down and ate a cheese sandwich with them. It was wonderful for their morale, and I could see the spirit of the crew pick up immediately."

At about 1 p.m., Tracy finished his sandwich and told Merrick, "I'm going back to the motel to take a nap." Said Merrick to me later, "Everything seemed just fine and dandy, so I sent him to Montrose in a company car and I stayed behind to finish some work. At 5 p.m., I returned to the hotel myself. Tracy's Thunderbird was gone. 'Mr. Tracy checked out at about three this afternoon,' the motel owner told me. 'He didn't leave any message.' "

This latest Tracy disappearance lasted for more than a week. Both Merrick and Wise kept calling the studio to find out if Tracy had gone back to Los Angeles to see producer Sam Zimbalist, but Zimbalist did not know where Tracy was, either.

"I didn't get too worried at that point," says director Wise, "because I knew Tracy was very anxious about a little cyst he had had removed from his face, and since he seemed very hypochondriacal about skin cancer, I gave him the benefit of the doubt and figured that he was seeing his dermatologist. I continued filming the scenes in which he did not appear. But I was beginning to get desperate. We had a bunkhouse that had been built into a Quonset hut, where we only were going to shoot in the event of bad weather. The weather was fine, but I did the bunkhouse scenes anyway, using Bob Francis and the ranch-hands."

Merrick was getting desperate, too. He told me,

"It was my job to keep the news from the world that Tracy was missing. I took the editor of the local newspaper into my confidence, and, every day, I wrote a front page story for him, just as if Tracy was there and working. I did stories about Tracy going to Denver for a weekend. Strickling told me to keep it up as long as possible, because Tracy's pattern was that he would eventually return. Strick told me his absence was costing the studio approximately thirty thousand dollars a day. That was the price of just keeping the company in the field. By now, close to two hundred thousand dollars had gone down the drain."

On 19 June, eight days after Tracy had left, Merrick suddenly got a call from Grand Junction, Colorado, about sixty miles away. It was Tracy, who by now had become accustomed to flying. "I just landed at the airport here," he said. "Can you send a car to get me?" Merrick sent the car and met Tracy when he arrived in Montrose. Without a word of explanation, Tracy said, "OK, now we're ready to get to work.

Reports director Wise,

"I went over to see him in his wing of the motel that night and he seemed fine. He avoided telling me where he'd been but said he was still worried about the removal of the cyst on his face. He had a quarter-inch patch on his cheek. When he removed it, I could see a tiny healed scar that was barely visible to the naked eye. Then he complained about the altitude. I reminded him that this is what he had insisted on, fresh green meadows high up in the mountains. 'Yeah,' he said. I said,

'OK, why don't you take it easy for the first few days until you get used to the altitude.' "

Merrick apparently didn't know about this concession by Wise. He told me,

"The next morning we went out to the location. Tracy got on his horse and played four scenes. He did each scene once. At the end of each take, he'd say to Wise, 'Well, that seemed all right to me. What's the next shot?' I felt he was taking charge of the production away from the director. When lunch-time came, Tracy said, 'I'm going to the motel,' and he quit for the day. He worked three half-days like that. At the motel, he refused to go out to eat and insisted that Arvid Griffen, one of the finest assistant directors in the business, cook for him on a hot plate in his room."

On the second day, Tracy said cryptically to Merrick, "Howard Strickling is in Denver." On the third day, Strickling was on the location, standing quietly behind the cameraman. Said Merrick,

"Tracy was doing a scene on horseback with Bob Francis. Tracy rode too fast and Francis dropped out of camera range. Wise called for a retake, but, instead, Tracy got off his horse and walked over to Strickling. He and Strickling walked into a trailer. They met together in the trailer for a while. Bobby Wise joined them. The next thing I knew, Tracy and Strickling were taking off down the mountain to Montrose in one car and Wise and his assistant director, Arvid Griffen, left the location in another car. Everyone looked pale."

This was the denouement that had been building up for weeks.

Says Wise,

"I don't remember anything about the Strickling and Tracy meeting in the trailer. All I know was that I was fed up with the most unpleasant period I had ever spent with a star. On the first day of work, Tracy complained constantly about the altitude. On the second day, he began to say it was too bad the location wasn't down lower, and that it should be moved down to six thousand feet.

"On the third day — and I remember this vividly — he was doing a scene where he had to bend over and look at a horse's hoof. He gasped and said, 'Look what happens to me, Bobby. Let's face it. You better take me out of this picture. I'm not going to be able to finish it.' At that point, I had had it up to the ears. I turned to Arvid Griffen and said,

'Let's go down the hill so I can talk to the studio. I'm just not going to get through the picture with this guy. All he wants is to move the entire location further down the mountain, which will cost the studio millions of dollars.'

"So I drove down to Montrose with Arvid, and Tracy and Strickling followed in another car, the way Jim Merrick told it. At the motel, Strickling and Tracy went into Tracy's quarters and Arvid and I went into mine. I called MGM and spoke with Sam Zimbalist. I told him about all of Tracy's complaints about the altitude and wanting to change the location. I said he didn't think he could finish the picture under these conditions. I told Zimbalist, 'I think we should replace him.' "

It was unheard of for a director to ask to replace a superstar of Tracy's magnitude, but Zimbalist calmly told Wise to stand by. Wise says, "In an hour, Zimbalist called back. He had spoken with Dore Schary and others at the studio and in MGM's New York headquarters by that time. Sam said, 'OK, he's out. We'll try to get hold of Gable to see if he'll do it. In the meantime, I'll call Tracy and notify him that he's off the picture.'

Continues Wise,

"Arvid went up to the location to dismiss the troops. Zimbalist called back to say that Gable wasn't available but they'd try for someone else. Arvid came back and went in to see Tracy. Arvid returned to my suite, and said, 'You'd better go over there. He's absolutely distraught, saying, "It's the end of my career, I'm finished, it's never happened to me before.' " I went over and spent a half hour with Tracy. Strickling was there, trying to reassure him. As angry as I was, I was moved by Tracy's emotion. He was in tears. The studio had had similar episodes with him, his disappearances and so forth, but they never had pulled the rug out from under him. This was the first time they had not taken his side and not backed him up. Even I found myself reassuring him that his career was not over."

But it *was,* at least at MGM. He never made another film at the studio he had helped build into the mightiest force in the motion picture industry over a period of twenty exciting years.

There were still some ironic aftermaths to the *Tribute to a Bad Man* episode. James Cagney agreed to do the film, but the company had to close down and wait until he finished another picture. During the months-long hiatus, the entire cast and crew went back to Los Angeles. While there, young Robert Francis, with nothing to do, decided to take flying lessons. He was tragically killed in the crash of his trainer plane.

Cagney did the picture, with Don Dubbins replacing Francis. Wise had to re-shoot all the scenes he had done with Francis while waiting for Tracy to show up. The movie was a critical and box-office success.

And as for Tracy, his very next film was *The Mountain,* for Paramount. *The Mountain* was filmed near Chamonix in the French Alps at twelve thousand feet.

Chapter Twenty

Time Magazine once wondered about the miracle of the amount of protection Tracy received from the press, with scarcely any mention of his many personal problems, and, for a long time, no mention at all of his relationship with Hepburn. The magazine found that incredible for Hollywood, a community that thrived on gossip and scandal.

The *Tribute to a Badman* incident is a perfect example of one way in which that miracle was accomplished. It is an illustration of the near-perfect methodology of the Howard Strickling public-relations machine in those days.

"The cast and crew had to hang around Montrose for a few weeks," Jim Merrick told me, "while we were waiting for the studio to send a replacement for Tracy. Strick told me that in no way was I to let out the news that

215

Tracy had been fired, or that the production had been shut down. So I wrote stories about Tracy judging plays at the local high school, or Tracy riding a stagecoach through town on the Fourth of July, or Tracy visiting a ranch to buy horses. At the public events, I'd substitute another actor from the cast and explain to the people that Mr. Tracy had had a difficult day and was busy studying his lines. The *Denver Post* picked up my stories from the local paper, and the Hollywood columnists picked up the stories from the *Denver Post*. As far as anyone knew, Tracy was there and working. I discouraged out of town reporters from coming to the location, saying 'Mr. Tracy is sorry about doing this, but the work here is so arduous that he has requested a closed set.' The local reporters were kept away, too. I had fixed it so that I was the *only* source of information."

When they got back to Hollywood, there were no leaks from the cast and crew because no one knew what had really happened, and Merrick had convinced them the hiatus was due to technical reasons, a necessary reconstruction at the location. By the time Cagney arrived, and the filming was resumed at Montrose, the press and public generally had forgotten about Tracy's previous involvement in the picture. Since there was no official announcement about it, only a few sharp reporters even picked up the fact that Tracy was gone from Metro completely. They liked Tracy so much that they played the story down. It wasn't anything like when Clark Gable left the studio over money matters a short time before.

This liking and respect the press felt for Tracy is the other reason for the lack of derogatory or implicating stories about him, according to Joe Hyams, then Hollywood columnist for the *New York Herald-Tribune*. Ex-MGM publicist Esmé Chandlee disagrees. "I think it was more a liking and respect for Kate Hepburn. No one wanted to hurt *her* with bad stories about Tracy." The ultimate result of both this fondness and MGM publicity policy was that there was a generalized blackout, almost a gentlemen's agreement that no one would ever mention the Hepburn-Tracy romance in print or on the air.

Tracy's overall policy with the press was to refuse interviews whenever possible. Ralph Bellamy says that he once phoned Tracy in New York and asked him to consent to an interview by a woman journalist friend of his. Tracy stormed back with, "You son of a bitch, you *know* I don't talk to writers," and slammed down the phone. There are a few notable examples of how he reacted when he was cornered at press conferences. To one young man who asked him what he looked for in scripts, he snarled, "Days off." To another's rather idiotic

217

question, "Mr. Tracy, what makes a woman attractive?" Tracy stared and said, "I'll give you exactly thirty seconds to think up another question." Then there was his famous rejoinder to a question that always bugged him: "What advice do you have for young actors?", the answer being "Learn your lines and don't bump into the furniture."

As acerbic and cruel as he could be with some reporters, there were many he liked and with whom he developed genuine friendships. Among them were columnists Joe Hyams, Bob Thomas and James Bacon.

Hyams says,

"I came to Hollywood for the *New York Herald-Tribune* in 1952, and the first friend I made in the movie colony was Humphrey Bogart. Bogie had a devilish sense of humour and he used to like to sic me onto people in the hopes that I would give them a hard time, which indeed I did. One of the first people he sent me to was Tracy, his very good friend. I saw Tracy on a movie set, and the first thing he told me was that he gave very few interviews; but since I had the Bogart seal of approval, he'd talk. He did, and after that, he never refused me an interview.

"Like Bogey, he was pixyish and liked to stir up trouble. He once told me exactly how much money Burt Lancaster was making in

Judgment at Nuremberg, and told me to check it with Burt. Spence's figure was right on the nose and it infuriated Lancaster that I knew it. In fact, I thought Burt was going to charge me and attack me on the set. Tracy, watching, just laughed and laughed and laughed.

"Spence was a witty and sentimental man. When Bogie was dying, I saw him at the Bogart house nearly every time I was there. Bogie, who had cancer, had shrunk down to about 80 pounds, and Betty, Lauren Bacall, would lower him in a dumbwaiter from his bedroom to the living room where he'd sip a couple of cocktails. Spence would cheer him up with stories, mostly gossip in the industry, and so would David Niven, Richard Burton, anyone who kept dropping in. When Bogie died at 2 a.m. one morning, Betty called me in the middle of the night and told me the last ones to see Bogie that afternoon were Tracy and Kate Hepburn. When I next saw Tracy, he was distraught, as he was later over the deaths of Gable and Marilyn Monroe.

"I think I got along so well with Tracy for two reasons. First, he respected my paper, which he read all the time. Secondly, I never talked about his drinking or his family. I didn't even know the name of his wife. As for Hepburn, I always saw them together and considered them like a married couple, with a lot of warmth between them, though I never mentioned her in connection with Tracy in my columns. After all, it was nip and tuck in those days, and none of us reporters wanted to be banned from the studios."

It was the same with Bob Thomas of the Associated Press, also a distinguished biographer, who says, "It wasn't the policy of the AP to print news about extramarital affairs. Even the affair between Marion Davies and William Randolph Hearst was not mentioned until much later. We couldn't afford to offend the studios. Also, we couldn't mention things like Tracy's drinking unless it appeared on a police blotter and the studios were very careful to avoid that."

Like Hyams, Thomas always had complete and friendly access to Tracy, until one day when he ran foul of him, an incident which Thomas has not discussed until now.

"I was on the set of *Judgment at Nuremberg*," relates Thomas, "and because there were so many stars around — Tracy, Burt Lancaster, Maximilian Schell, Judy Garland, Marlene Dietrich, Monty Clift — I though up a provocative question to ask Lancaster, my first interview. I put it in a kidding way, saying, 'You're dealing with a lot of ham here. How do you handle it?' My whimsy seems to have escaped Lancaster, who has no sense of humour. I was hoping he would respond in kind but he didn't respond at all. I just shrugged it off.

"But when I returned to the set a few days later and said hello to Tracy, he responded gruffly with, 'What the hell are you doing here?' I went over to talk with Judy Garland and Tracy shouted, 'Watch out for that guy. He's poison.' I interviewed Max Schell and went back to Tracy. To my surprise, he was really incensed. He said, 'I suppose you've come around to talk to the hams.' He turned his back on me and I walked off the set. I was not thrown off the set, as some reports have it, but for a long time I didn't have any contact at all with Tracy, with whom I'd been quite close. It wasn't until six years later that I was at a Tracy press conference and he said, 'I get along with the press. Thomas and I had a little thing going, but it's over now.' *He* had decided it was over and now we were to have good relations again."

Another good friend of Tracy's in journalism was James Bacon, originally with Associated Press but later a columnist with *The Hollywood Reporter* and the *Los Angeles Herald Examiner*. Bacon, too, had a contretemps which interrupted the relationship, but this time the flap was with Hepburn rather than Tracy.

Says Bacon:

"I had done some heavy drinking with Gable
and Tracy in the old days, but I didn't know
much about Spence's major binges because
Howard Strickling kept the news of them
pretty much under control. The AP wouldn't
use the stories, anyway. Jim Backus told me
it was good to work in a Tracy picture because there always was three weeks extra work
while Tracy went off on a tear. But I never
used stuff like that in my column. So he had
a drinking problem, that's it. Everybody
drank."

So Bacon and Tracy remained good friends for
fifteen years, with Bacon only writing news from
the set type stories. But, in 1963, Bacon wandered
into the old Romanoff's Restaurant on Rodeo
Drive in Beverly Hills and espied Tracy sitting at
the bar.

"That surprised me," says Bacon, "because
Tracy was sick and supposed to be on the
wagon, and I knew that he never drank in
public places. But I went over and he invited
me to have a drink. We had several. Then he
invited me to have lunch and we kept drinking at lunch. All of a sudden, his head fell

right down into the mashed potatoes he was eating. He was out cold. I moved his head so he wouldn't smother in the mashed potatoes and I called Mike Romanoff over.

"I said to Mike, 'Have a couple of your men help me get him out to my car. I'll drive him home. I know where he lives.' I knew because, just a few days before, a publicity man name Frank McFadden had told me he'd leased his Trancas Beach house to Hepburn and Tracy. So we got Tracy in my car—he was a dead weight—and I drove him to hell and gone all the way to Trancas Beach, about fifteen miles up the coast, beyond Malibu.

"When I got there, I dragged Tracy out of the car. He was still out cold and pretty heavy because he had gained a lot of weight. Kate came out from behind the house and said, 'God damn you, you've always been an evil companion for Spence.' She was madder'n hell. She bent down and I thought she might be looking for a brick to throw at me, so I dropped Tracy in a dead heap and got in my car and drove away. I didn't see Spence after that, and the next time I saw Kate, she was on location for a picture in France, *The Madwoman of Chaillot,* and she still wouldn't speak to me."

My own experiences with Tracy were always

pleasant and uncluttered. As he did with Joe Hyams, he respected the publication I worked for, *LOOK* magazine, and he gave me all the time I needed when I was assigned to do a profile of him. We had chatted amiably on the set of *Inherit the Wind,* and I had watched him perform one of the greatest feats of screen acting I'd ever seen; his summation to the jury, eleven minutes of monologue in one take, without a single fluff or break in the action. The entire crew and cast applauded, including Fredric March and Gene Kelly.

I wanted a long interview session with Tracy and he suggested that we have dinner together at Chasen's Restaurant. When I got there, I was surprised to be ushered up to a private second-floor room which ordinarily was used only for cocktail parties. Tracy was at a table in the center of the otherwise-unoccupied room. He was with a young press agent, Pat Newcombe (now a film executive), who I suspected was there at the behest of Kate Hepburn, as Tracy did not have a paid publicist of his own.

We were served in solitary splendour by three of Chasen's waiters and Tracy ate only sparingly. He drank only water. He amazed me by bringing up the two taboo subjects, his drinking and Hepburn, and speaking openly and frankly about both.

Concerning his drinking, he actually used the word "alcoholic." He said,

224

"I began to wonder a long time ago about why some people could hold their liquor and some couldn't. Gable, for instance, could booze all night and it never showed. With me, I could take just a couple of drinks and all kinds of terrible things happened to me. I'd go into blackouts and wake up in some goddam distant city. At first I thought it was that all Irishmen were drunks, but now I realize that's a slander on my heritage. Now I think maybe it's genetic. My father was a heavy drinker and so is my brother Carroll. He spends every afternoon at the bar at the Bistro here in Beverly Hills."

(Tracy was fifteen years ahead of his time. Now, the genetic theory of alcoholism is gaining more and more medical credence in the field, with several scientific studies tending to point in that direction.)

Said Tracy,

"At first I thought it all started with me over my shock and disappointment when my son, John, was born deaf. Now I realize that was all bullshit. I was drinking long before that. We're always looking for excuses. I even found an excuse for going on a binge when John got divorced in 1957. When I came out of it, I said to myself, 'What the hell. The

225

kid has done wonderful things with his life, being an artist at the Disney studios, and all. So his life did get screwed up. So what? Look at all the other things in him I've got to be proud of.' "

A good deal of Tracy's problem about his son's divorce was its handling in the press. Protected for years by his studio's influence in the media, Tracy did not seem to understand the plight of the ordinary citizen, whose statements and documents in court can be printed verbatim as "privileged information." Thus, when Nadine testified that "John repulsed me after the birth of Joey . . . If I put my arm around him, he would say 'Let me alone' . . . He treated me like a servant"; and when John testified that his only income was from trust funds and one hundred dollars a week, gifts from his father, Tracy, according to George Cukor, did not understand that these were typical court-room exaggerations to gain advantage, and became infuriated with what he considered to be exaggerations by the *press*.

As far as his being proud of John, Tracy made his pride abundantly clear. He said,

"With all the medical problems the kid had when he was young, I saw him develop into quite an athlete. I took him with me when I played polo, and he got up on a horse, and soon he was one of the best polo players at the club. I also watched him develop into a championship swimmer in school. He couldn't hear the starter's gun, but he picked up a sixth sense, maybe from the vibration of the shot, and I never saw him make a false start. We're very close. He even came to see me when I was doing *The Rugged Path* on the stage in New York. I put him in the front row and he could read my lips and understand every word I said. Knowing that, I put on my best performance of the run."

Tracy shook his head sadly. He said, "Unfortunately, John's not feeling too well these days. He's coming down with something all the time."

(John Tracy, indeed, became chronically ill from a variety of ailments, requiring constant attention from his mother, Louise, much as she had had to do when he was a child.)

Tracy was equally proud of Susie. He said, "Would you believe it, but that little button wrote herself the cutest little book about a little girl teaching a deaf cat to cope, and she got it published. And she's also turning into one helluva little photographer. She's as close to John as a sister can be, and when he's sick, she takes care of him just as good as Louise does."

But most of Tracy's praise was heaped on Hepburn. His pride constantly showed throughout the entire conversation.

He spoke of her as, "Kate, my Kate," and only occasionally, with gruff affection, "my bag of bones." He said, "I don't care what the Academy thought when they gave the Oscar to Vivien Leigh. In *African Queen* that year, my bag of bones turned in one of the greatest performances I've seen anywhere."

He said, "My Kate really has me pegged. She told Stanley Kramer that I'm much too impatient for the time and place in which I find myself."

Tracy spoke warmly of the many loving things they did together.

"We were in Paris," he said, "and she suddenly decided we were going to take a long walk."

" 'How much of a walk?' " I said.

'We'll go up the Champs Elysees, down to the Seine, and then all the way along the river to Notre Dame.'

" 'Nuts to that,' I said. 'You're a country girl. I can't walk that far.' But my Kate runs me and we walked. At the Cathedral, she wanted to walk back. I said, 'I'm taking a cab.' I got in the cab and after a few blocks I turned him around and found Kate again. 'OK,' I said, 'What are we going to do now, you tireless bag of bones?' She said, 'We're going to walk through the Louvre until it closes.' We did, too. And I never even thought of having a glass of wine at all the cafés we passed along the way."

Having come from the East, and not knowing all the Hollywood taboos about never mentioning the Tracy-Hepburn relationship, and not having been admonished by either Tracy or Ms. Newcombe *not* to mention it, I included some of what Tracy had told me in my *LOOK* article.

I was immediately excoriated by writers in Hollywood. One author wrote in a book, "It took Hepburn six months to get over the Davidson article." Another wrote, "Davidson was crossed off certain Hollywood invitations lists" (which I was never on).

But then *everyone* was writing about Tracy and Hepburn in the few remaining years of his life.

Chapter Twenty-one

Even in his anger at Tracy after having to fire him from *Tribute to a Bad Man,* Robert Wise says, "I've studied the man's work and his talent as an actor was unique and wonderful. He had that rare magic that could grab you the moment he appeared on the screen. No one could underplay, like he did, with a line, or even just a look."

Columnist James Bacon recalls the following conversation between Sir Laurence Olivier and Tracy at one of those bibulous afternoons at Humphrey Bogart's house when Bogie was dying:

Olivier: "Spencer, you *are* the greatest living actor."

Tracy: "Fuck you, you limey bastard, you're the greatest living actor."

Olivier: "All right, then, I'll amend my statement. In view of your unwillingness to try anything more challenging on the stage, *you're* the greatest living *screen* actor."

Perhaps the highest tribute to Tracy's talent comes from James Cagney:

"Sure he was a fallible human being, but what counts is what he did on the screen. There was only one Garbo and there was only one Tracy. He left an unusual monument to himself in his own lifetime. Do you notice how mimics and comedians are always imitating me and other actors. Well, nobody imitates Tracy. Nobody *can* imitate Tracy. What other actor can you say that about?"

Tracy himself downplayed his own acting talent, saying, "Shit, it's only a job, which I worked at and learned how to do pretty well, just by learning my lines."

There is no actor, living or dead, who ever agreed with that self-assessment. Orson Welles said, "The camera is kind to some people, but with Spence, it was more of a symbiotic relationship between him and the camera. The lens picked up every emotion he played. You could *see* him thinking."

Gene Kelly says, "Some actors work from the teeth. Everything Spence did came from inside.

He's one of the few people about whom you could say, 'He had a *God*-given talent.' "

Aside from those few actors he deliberately threw off stride—Rex Williams, Irene Papas, Robert Francis—there was only one who ever complained about working with Tracy. And that was not Tracy's fault. The actor was Jack Oakie, with whom Tracy did a terrible picture called *Looking for Trouble* in 1934. It is not generally known, but Oakie was deaf. He was too vain to wear a hearing aid, and the only reason he was so successful in films for so many years was that, like young John Tracy, he was an expert lip-reader.

"Tracy threw me completely," said Oakie. "He was so fantastically good and underplaying, emphasizing key lines with just a meaningful mumble, that I got hopelessly screwed up. I couldn't read his lips because he hardly moved them at all when he mumbled, so a lot of the time, I didn't know what the fuck he was saying. Not taking anything away from Spence's talent, it was a very rough experience for me, and I never agreed to work with him again."

There are many actors and actresses, on the other hand, who never worked with Tracy at all, but who gained great knowledge from just watching him. That was true of many of the young players at Metro Goldwyn Mayer. One of them was June Allyson, who came to MGM in 1943 when she was twenty-six years old. Says Miss Allyson, "When Tracy was working and we had nothing else to do, the kids at Metro, like Van Johnson and me, would go over to his set and hang around behind the camera just to study his techniques. It was a great learning experience."

Even Kate Hepburn, eight years older than Miss Allyson, watched Tracy work, with fascination, long before they met and did their first film together in 1942. Like many others, she was particularly struck by his enormous powers of concentration. In an interview with writer Roy Newquist she said,

"Well, Spencer Tracy just *is*. He is the most remarkable actor ever born. He is one of the few people capable of total concentration. When you watch him, on the screen or on the stage, you are simply present at something. It's a happening. It has nothing to do with apparent planning, yet it is the result of total concentration. Spencer will read the script over and over again, but he doesn't decide, as some actors do, 'I'm going to lift my hand and scratch my nose at this point.' In the first place, he wouldn't understand how you were going to reach up and scratch your nose until you found out what the other fellow was going to do in the scene."

Richard Widmark put it to me in another way, in perhaps the most succinct discussion I have had concerning Tracy's greatness as an actor. Says Widmark,

"Tracy had the greatest concentration of any actor I've ever seen, and concentrating on a movie set is one of the most difficult things to accomplish because of all the peripheral and mechanical things going on around you. Tracy was able to shut himself off from all this while he was doing a scene. The set could fall down, and it wouldn't bother him. He was playing the guy he was playing, and that was it. Stanley Kramer knew that, and that's why Stanley gave Spence a long ten or eleven minute scene, all by himself, in practically every picture he made for him. Stanley realized that very few actors in the world could pull off such a feat on the screen."

Like Gene Kelly, Widmark firmly believes that Tracy's talent was God-given.

"It was a built-in capability, something that came along with him from the time he was a very young man; so from the very beginning, he was way ahead of most of the pack. I know, because I used to watch his movies from the time I was a kid in Minnesota, and long before I entered this business. I learned more from studying Spence on the screen than I could in any acting class. Amazingly, he was just as good in *Up the River* in 1930 as he was in *Guess Who's Coming to Dinner* in 1967. Olivier, on the other hand, had to work like hell to develop as an actor, from what I could see in *his* early films. He wasn't too good then, but Olivier *made* himself into a great, great actor.

"The difference between Tracy and Olivier, who works everything out in great detail, was that Spence was a very instinctive actor. It just came to him. It was nothing he had planned. He just seemed to know how human beings would react under certain conditions that would crop up in a play or a screen play, and would duplicate those reactions with unfailing authenticity. Maybe it was because he had a writer's or an artist's eye to record the looks and feelings of the common man, with whom he grew up. In a way, it was too easy for him. God knows what heights he would have achieved as an actor if he had had to work harder. We all know how Olivier kept urging him to go to England with him to do Shakespeare, and how Spence kept turning him down. But he always was proud of just the fact that Olivier wanted him to do it."

Widmark was in two films with Tracy, *Broken Lance* and *Judgment at Nuremberg*. In all, he and Tracy got along extremely well. Tracy believed that the first take of a scene was always the best. "So do I," says Widmark, "if everything else works with the sound man, the camera man, the other technicians. In the first take, the adrenaline is flowing, you're nervous, you're up. The director wasn't always too happy about that and would order another take. Tracy would say, 'Why?' But if it was explained to him reasonably, he'd do it. Spence and I were in harmony on that."

They were in harmony on other things, too. For one thing, neither could stand unprofessionalism in actors.

"When we began *Judgment at Nuremberg,*" says Widmark, "Tracy told me that he had just finished a picture, in Hawaii, *The Devil at Four O'Clock* and that 'I got tired of acting with a broomstick.' What that meant was that his co-star, Frank Sinatra, refused to stand out of camera range and read his lines so that Tracy could respond in close-ups. Instead, a script girl would read the lines while someone held up a broomstick to establish eye-level, at which Tracy would direct his gaze. This would be the spot from which Sinatra supposedly was talking to him. Spence and I both agreed that Sinatra's refusal to read was unprofessional. In our picture, Spence and I would both stay on the set as long as necessary to read off-camera for the benefit of whatever actor was being shot in close-up.

"We also agreed that doing a picture is something like being in the Army: a certain amount of griping is necessary, and we both did it. Most of the time, Spence was affable with me and other members of the cast, but occasionally he got moody and wanted to be by himself. I could understand that because I get moody, too. I could also understand his blowing his stack when an actor goofed off or started fooling around, getting in Spence's line-of-sight while he was doing a scene. Another thing I could understand. We discussed why he so frequently didn't like the pictures he worked in, and I came to believe he was embarrassed about being an actor as an older man. I realized that I was beginning to feel the same way, saying to myself, 'Jesus, this is a trade for kids.'

"What I remember most of all is how Tracy's brilliance as an actor pulled *me* up as an actor. I had gone into *Broken Lance* with bad feelings. It was my last picture at Fox. Darryl Zanuck was teed off at me, so he put me in this picture, giving me fourth or fifth billing. He was angry because I didn't want to re-sign with the studio. I didn't want to do the movie and tried to get out of it. So I wasn't in a very good frame of mind when I was forced to go to the location in Nogales, Arizona. My inclination was to just walk through the picture, collect my money and get out.

"But all that changed as soon as I began to work with Tracy. He was so brilliant, even in this unimportant little film, that I couldn't just walk through it. I had to call on all my acting skills and work my ass off, just to keep up with him. It was so enjoyable working with him. We'd really go at each other, and he gave me so much to make me come out at my best. As a result, I ended up with some pretty damned fine reviews for my fourth-or-fifth-billed role. I remember one review in *Newsweek* saying, in effect, that the picture was saved and the intensity created 'by a couple of eminently competent craftsmen, Spencer Tracy and Richard Widmark.' "

Widmark says that only twice in his career did he ask for autographed photos of stars he worked with. The first actor was Lionel Barrymore, with whom he did *Down to the Sea in Ships*. The second was Tracy, who refused to sign the picture Widmark brought him, saying he looked too old. Nevertheless, Widmark still has the unsigned Tracy photograph hanging in his study.

However, as in all episodes involving Tracy, the enigma, the dark side of him emerged at least once.

Says Widmark,

"About a week into the picture, Spence was doing a scene in the middle of a little stream on the location. I wasn't in the scene. I was just hanging around, watching him work. But apparently I must have gotten into the wrong place because he held up the action and roared at me, 'Who the fuck do you think's the star of this picture?'

"With all his good qualities, Spence was not exactly Humble Sam."

Chapter Twenty-two

Tracy *was* Humble Sam for a while, after his firing both from *Tribute to a Bad Man* and from MGM. But, with Hepburn's encouragement, he accepted his new role as a freelance actor, and did *not* go off on the alcoholic binge expected by his friends. In fact, he began to look forward with great excitement to his next picture, *The Mountain,* which he had negotiated in a deal with Paramount. He did not anticipate that the film would bring him his closest brush with death since he began his acting career some thirty-five years before.

He had no premonition of this, of course, and he attacked the pending project with unusual enthusiasm. He had read and optioned the novel on which the movie was based and greatly admired the novelist, Henri Troyat, who, he told Robert Wagner, "is as good as Ernest Hemingway"—an opinion not shared by literary critics nor borne out by subsequent history. Tracy was also pumped up by the fact that the producer-director of the film was to be Edward Dmytryk, who had done *Crossfire* and *The Caine Mutiny,* and who had directed Tracy without alteration in *Broken Lance.* Unlike his days at Metro, Tracy was consulted fully by Dmytryk on most matters of pre-production, including casting.

The story was a simple one. Zachary Teller, a gentle, kindly Alpine mountain guide, has a ne'er-do-well younger brother, Chris, whom he is trying to rear in the ways of righteousness. The action centers on a plane crash high in the mountains. Chris wants to climb the mountain to loot the plane wreckage and old Zachary, who is against the idea, goes along with Chris just to make sure his head-strong brother doesn't get killed in the climb. The plane victims' bodies are plundered by Chris, but Zachary saves the one survivor, a Hindu girl, from Chris's murderous intent, and builds a sled to carry her down the mountain. Brother Chris, laden with stolen valuables, follows and is killed in a fall.

Not quite Hemingway, but a serviceable action-adventure plot for the tastes of 1956.

What interested Tracy most was that he was successful in getting Dmytryk and Paramount to cast Robert Wagner as the brother, Chris, an anomaly for the screen, as Tracy was then fifty-six and Wagner twenty-six, making them siblings born a rather improbable thirty years apart. No matter. Tracy had developed a great fondness for Wagner, and, as a sort of surrogate father for the young man, wanted to do everything he could to advance his career. Wagner, in turn, had idolized Tracy since he was twelve years old.

Says Wagner,

"In the 1930s, my father kept some horses at the Riviera Club and I used to go there to shovel shit and to watch the movie stars play polo. Spence was one of the polo players. I was star-struck, like most kids growing up in Los Angeles, and I wanted to become a movie actor some day. So I went to see every picture I could, and Tracy always was the best in my eyes. Even then, I could see the beauty of his work in how he made difficult things seem so simple. Also, his skill in using every prop and person on the set as a take-off for unusual things he wanted to do.

"I didn't actually meet Spence until I was under contract to 20th and had done a picture called *Beneath the 12-Mile Reef*. I got a Golden Globe that year as the Most Promising Newcomer, and, for some reason, Spence was at the awards. He told me he liked my work in *Beneath the 12-Mile Reef*, and we talked a while, and suddenly he said, 'Kid, I want you to play my son, Joe, in a picture I've got coming up, *Broken Lance*.' All I could say to myself was 'Wow! *Me* in a picture with the man I considered the greatest actor in the world.' The man I considered the *second* greatest, Clark Gable, said to me, 'Kid, when you work with Spence hold on to anything you can; he'll blow you away.'

"But it didn't work out that way on the set, even though he was his usual cantankerous self when I said, 'Maybe I'm too young for this part?' and he said, 'Stick around, boy. We'll age you.' He couldn't have been more kind to me, teaching me a lot about acting that has stood me in good stead to this day. A couple of years later, he asked for me again, for *The Mountain,* and he insisted that my name should be above the title, like his. Humphrey Bogart said, 'Name above the title? That's ridiculous. It's something you should work for years to earn.' I was pretty brash then and I said to Bogie, 'Well, if you were working in *my* picture, I'd put *your* name above the title.' "

Tracy and Wagner left for France to begin work on *The Mountain.* They spent a few days in Paris, and Wagner says it was the most educational period of his career: "He introduced me to a lot of important people, and to great works of art, and to great works of literature. He told me, 'You've got to read the classics, kid, if you want to be a good actor.' "

Strangely, Tracy was doing with Wagner what Hepburn had done with him.

They finally reached the location headquarters at

Chamonix, in the French Alps, beneath the bulk of the 15,771-foot Mont Blanc. Chamonix itself was at three thousand feet; the filming sites ranged up to fourteen thousand feet. Wagner says, "The sight of the mountains saddened Spence. He was still feeling badly about what had happened on *Tribute to a Bad Man*. Up here, though, I never heard him complain once about the altitude. It was difficult for all of us to breathe."

The crotchety side of Tracy showed up on the first day, when director Dmytryk introduced him to the make-up man, Frank Westmore, one of the famous Westmore brothers who were considered the leading experts in their field. As Westmore related the incident, which took place at the Hotel des Alpes,

"I knew I was in some trouble when Tracy started a diatribe against make-up men. He said, he didn't want or need make-up, adding, 'My face looks like a shithouse door and nothing can help it, not even a Westmore.' "

Said Frank, "I replied with some heat, 'Mr. Tracy, I'm here to be of some help to anyone who needs my services. If you don't want any make-up, I couldn't care less.' Dmytryk's eyes indicated that I'd be on the next plane back to the States. So did Tracy's. He said, 'You arrogant son-of-a-bitch, take your cap off when you yell at me.'

245

" 'I can't take my goddam cap off,' I screamed back, 'because I look like a goddam Mohican.'

"With that, I whipped off the cap, revealing a two-inch-wide bald strip down the middle of my head. I had bought a French gadget to trim my own hair, and, not being able to read French, had put the cutting edge in backwards. Tracy cracked up and so did Dmytryk. For the rest of the movie, I had no further trouble with Spencer Tracy."

Wagner says,

"Spence worked hard when we finally got going, and there was only the usual amount of griping from him. It was a tough location. There was deep snow everywhere. We had experienced mountain climbers to guide us, but we had to wear crampon spikes on our boots, and layer after layer of clothing to help us survive the bitter cold. Dmytryk saw to it that most of Spence's scenes were done at lower levels, if you can call twelve thousand feet lower levels. He was never required to go up to our main location, the very top of Aiguille du Midi, which at twelve thousand feet, is one of the highest peaks in the Alps. The only way to reach it was by funicular cable car from Chamonix. The first time *I* had to go up to

246

Aiguille du Midi, I have to admit I was very nervous. When I tell you I only saw the sweet side of Spence, this should prove it. He said, 'I know I don't have to go up there, but I know how scared you are, so I'll go along with you in the fuckin' cable car.' "

This particular funicular, a car suspended from a single cable, was, at that time at least, the longest in the world. At midpoint, the car was a mile above the terrain below.

"When we got close to midpoint," says Wagner, "we felt a terrible jolt, and the car began swinging free, to and fro. It swung so far forward that the front windshield hit the cable and shattered. The below zero cold came rushing in. I was sure I was going to die, and from the look on Spence's face and the French driver's, I know they felt they were finished, too.

"Then we stopped swinging, and, for the moment at least, it didn't look as if we were going to take that one-mile plunge to the rocks below. So now we focused our attention on the possibility of our freezing to death. The driver told us that the car's wheels had slipped the cable, and we were just hanging by God-knows-what. Eventually he was told by radio that an open work-car was coming down from above to take us off. But then, when the work car arrived, we figured it would be impossible to get Spence out on the roof of *our* car, to transfer him to the workcar. I felt that if we tried, he certainly would have slipped or rolled off, and plunged to his death.

"Then, after what seemed like ages in the numbing cold—actually it was about two hours—the work car began pushing us backwards. By some miracle, the wheels on our car engaged the cable again. But we couldn't go down. We had to go all the way up to the Aiguille de Midi, and *then* all the way down again. Spence was white as a sheet. I'm sure I was, too. When we reached the cable station down below, crew members helped Spence off to his hotel room, and I staggered to mine. The whole thing was such a nightmare that I can't blame Spence for what he did that night."

Refusing to say anything derogatory about Tracy, Wagner declines to relate what he did that night, but make-up man Frank Westmore reported it in detail in a book, *The Westmores of Hollywood,* which he co-wrote with my late wife.
Said Westmore:

"I had to pack up my gear, so I left the mountaintop later. The funicular now was working fine. When I arrived at our hotel, Tracy was in the bar sitting at a small table, well on his way to drinking himself into a stupor. Wagner and I joined him. Strangely, he was very talkative and friendly, actually charming, telling all sorts of fascinating Hollywood stories, even as his head sagged lower and lower on his chest. He ordered another round of drinks.

"I was sure this would be the one that would put him away and we could haul him off to bed, when suddenly, without reason, Tracy picked up his empty brandy snifter and hurled it at the approaching waiter's face. Wagner put up his right hand to catch the snifter before it hit the waiter. His hand closed reflexively over the glass, which shattered in his fist and cut his two middle fingers to the bone. Wagner's blood splattered all over the place. Tracy was oblivious to everything by then and didn't even know that he was being wrestled from his chair by members of the crew and hustled up to his room. I helped our company doctor as he stitched and bandaged Wagner's hand, meanwhile pondering the practical consideration of how I could mask the gashes for the remainder of the film.

"The next morning I fished around in my make-up box and found a bottle of collodion. This is a colorless liquid, actually acid-treated cotton fibers dissolved in a mixture of ether and alcohol which I sometimes use to create an artificial scar on an actor's face. I knew that collodion is antiseptic and is also used in the boxing ring, between rounds, to seal bad facial cuts sustained by prizefighters. So that morning (and for the rest of the movie) I applied collodion to Wagner's hand and covered it with make-up after it dried, neatly obliterating the stitches. A contrite Tracy watched the procedure, barely remembering what had happened the night before."

Tracy was unusually tranquil for the rest of the filming in the Alps (the picture was completed with an artificial mountainside built on a sound stage in Hollywood). The crew soon found out the reason for their star's benignity and the fact that he totally abstained from drinking any more liquor. The reason was the appearance of a young woman named Margaret Shipway, a very proper, tweed-clad, upper-class British lady. Said Westmore,

"At first, we thought she was Tracy's secretary, but then it turned out that she actually was *Hepburn's* secretary. Kate had sent Miss Shipway to our location to keep an eye on Tracy and help him stay on an even keel. Maggie, as we called her, did a good job, even filling in as script clerk for a while. Thus, she could keep an eye on Tracy even while he was out working in the snow and rocks."

The filming was completed without further incident and the picture was released later in that year, 1956. It did not fare too well, either with the public or the critics, many of whom noted that it was ludicrous to keep thinking of Tracy as Wagner's brother throughout the film, when he actually looked like Wagner's grandfather. Tracy sulked, but there was no time for the sulking to become destructive. He signed almost immediately to do his seventh film with Hepburn, *Desk Set*. Now Kate could keep an eye on him *herself*.

As for Wagner, he considers *The Mountain* the most exciting experience of his career, despite the reviews. He says,

"Just being with Spence and learning from him every day was the most important thing that ever happened to me. We did many more scenes together than we had in *Broken Lance,* and I was entranced watching the master at work. Those were the days of the Actor's Studio and 'the Method', when everybody sat around on the stage analyzing everything. Spence didn't analyze. He came to work so very well prepared, and then figured out how to use the props, the set, even *me,* to enrich his performance. He made it look so natural, so very easy. He took it down to the basics. He looked like he was doing nothing, but he had tremendous power, tremendous power. I often wondered why there never has been a Tracy cult, like there's a Humphrey Bogart cult. Maybe it's because Spence was so good, he made it look *too* easy. He never had to be flashy to get the power into his performance. I once asked him to teach me that wonderful technique of underplaying, which he had mastered. He said, 'Forget the tricks, kid. Just stick to learning the basics, and you'll develop your own tricks as you go along.' "

Tracy and Wagner remained very close friends long after *The Mountain,* which was the last film they did together. The relationship was an extraordinary one, considering Tracy's curmudgeonlike attitude toward most people in his latter days. It represents the *good* side of Tracy, at its best.
Wagner says,

"He loved my wife, Natalie, and visited with us a lot. I have photos of Spence cutting the cake at my thirtieth birthday party. When Natalie and I divorced and I moved to Europe, Spence frequently came over and stayed with me. When I married again, to Marion Donen, he was at the wedding. He came out to our ranch here in California and was wonderful with our daughter, Katie. I visited him in his little house on the George Cukor estate, and I don't know how many people he'd even let in there."

Wagner says that this continuing association with Tracy "changed my attitude, changed my work, changed my life." Wagner amplifies:

"He made me read and he made me *think* more. He developed my self-esteem, just by the fact that Spencer Tracy was interested in me. He constantly guided my career. It was Spence, in fact, who talked me into going into television, just at the right time, by saying, 'You've got to keep working and learning all the time.' So I ended up doing my first TV series, *It Takes a Thief,* and I eventually got to be a bigger star in television than I ever was in movies."

Idolatry? Yes. Unusual? Also yes. Aside from Hepburn, and his love for his two children whom he had left behind with wife Louise, Tracy was pretty much of a loner after fifty. Perhaps his relationship with Wagner fulfilled further basic paternal yearnings which had always been part of his makeup. If so, Wagner is a good son. He will say nothing about Tracy's dark side, or his drinking, or the glaring contradictions of his life. Wagner, also, will not discuss Hepburn, with whom he became very close, too.

Except: "Kate was the best thing that ever happened to Spence, with her wit, her charm, her intellect, her beauty, her compassion. In fact, Kate would be the best thing that could happen to *any* man."

Chapter Twenty-three

Edward Dmytryk, the director of *The Mountain,* has some startlingly different points of view from Wagner's about Tracy in that film, but he certainly agrees with him about the Tracy-Hepburn relationship.

Dmytryk tells a story about how he and Tracy first arrived in London on their way to Chamonix, met up with Hepburn, who was on her way to Australia, and dined in a restaurant in Soho with their friend, US Ambassador Lewis Douglas. "Katie was so cute," says Dmytryk, "because she had on kind of a long dress—almost a costume—and she looked like a little old lady from New England. And she was so charming, which amazed me because she can come on so strong.

"I remember she ate snails that night and reeked of garlic, which didn't faze her at all.

In fact, we all laughed about it. Then we walked all the way back to the Claridge Hotel, where Spence and I were staying. We went up to Spence's room. He took off his coat and lay down on the couch, saying he had some sort of problem with his neck. Without saying a word, Kate gave him a very professional massage of his neck. Then she made him some coffee. It was absolutely amazing to me how she took such good care of him, because this woman, who could be so tough on everybody, was so tender and solicitous with him. He just sat there like the lord of the manor while she ministered to him.

"Later, I took her back to her hotel, which was the Connaught, down the street. She never stayed in the same hotel with Spence and we even used the freight elevator to leave Claridge's, so she wouldn't be seen. The freight-elevator man knew her well and apparently had been taking her up and down for years, whenever she and Spence were in London. There was something so sweet and ingenuous about it. Spence later showed me a letter she had written him from Australia, and it was like a love letter between two twenty-year-olds."

This episode is not too startling because it coincides with what George Cukor and others have said.

Dmytryk, however, comes up with some other observations which do not agree with what previously has been stated about Tracy by nearly all friends, acquaintances, and by Tracy himself. There is the subject of why Tracy and Hepburn never married, for example. Dmytryk's wife is Jean Porter, a former MGM actress, and, says Dmytryk, "Jean just up and asked Spence one day, 'Is it really because you're Catholic?' "

" 'Hell, no,' he said. " 'When we first started going together, Katie wanted to get married. But my son, John, still was living at home and I felt that until he grew up and could take care of himself, I couldn't do it. Later, when all that cleared up, I wanted to marry Katie, but by that time she didn't want to marry *me*.' "

"That was straight out of Tracy's mouth. My wife is one of the few people I know who can ask a question like that, and get away with it."

Another totally unorthodox view from Dmytryk concerns Tracy's political attitudes. Many others, including Gene Kelly, say that Tracy was a right-wing conservative, or, at the very least, apolitical but leaning to the right. "Not so," says Dmytryk, who was imprisoned for his left-wing views during the Hollywood Ten inquisitions.

"Spence was generally liberal, generally sympathetic to people overall. He did *Broken Lance* with me, which was about racial intolerance, and while we were shooting in Arizona, he stayed with Supreme Court Justice William O. Douglas, a decided liberal. Clark Gable was right-wing, and so was Dick Powell, but not Tracy. In England, Ambassador Douglas, a Democrat, told us at dinner how Eisenhower had called him and asked him what should be done about the Joe McCarthy menace. Spence came across as definitely *not* a fan of McCarthy's. If he were, he couldn't have worked with me. He may have been different earlier in his life, but, as others have said, I'm sure Kate's influence helped."

In the making of the film *The Mountain,* Dmytryk, on the other hand, was witness to some of the same aspects of the dark side of Tracy that had been experienced by others. First came a repetition of that strange lack of confidence and the self-doubt that occurred every time Tracy started on a new project.

Says Dmytryk,

"*He* had bought the novel on which *The Mountain* was based; *he* had wanted to do it so badly that he screwed up on other pictures like *Tribute to a Bad Man; he* had so much confidence in me that he'd insisted to Paramount that I do the picture as both producer and director. Yet, just as we were all set to fly to England together and then go on to France, he came into my office and said, 'Eddie, I don't think I like this part.' I couldn't believe it, though I'd heard he'd done this before. He actually wanted to get out of the film which he had so painstakingly put together himself. He said, 'Goddamit, Clark isn't doing anything. Gable would be great in this part.' I said, 'I don't want Gable. You're the guy for this.' He said, 'I can't go. I just can't go.'

"It was then I realized that he probably was afraid of making such a long transatlantic plane flight. But maybe not. He *had* made trips like this with Hepburn before. So I cancelled our departure for a few days, and I said, 'Spence, if you're not there, I'm going to send two policemen, and they're going to pick you up, and *put you on the plane.*' I couldn't do that, of course, but I *did* send the production manager to fetch Spence and he got on the plane with no protest."

It was the same old pattern for Tracy. Once he started actual work on the film, his enthusiasm for the project returned.

Unfortunately, his alcoholic propensities returned, too, after the incident on the funicular cable car, when, in a drunken rage, he accidentally cut Robert Wagner's hand with the thrown brandy glass. Though his memory of the details differs slightly from Wagner's and make-up man Frank Westmore's, Dmytryk completely confirms the occurrence. He also confirms what we already know, that Tracy's form of alcoholism made him a periodic, rather than a steady drinker. "He didn't drink at all on *Broken Lance,*" says Dmytryk.

The director, who made so many noteworthy films, and now teaches at the American Film Institute, muses philosophically about alcoholism among movie actors. He says,

"It seems to me that I've worked with every damn drunk in the business, and most of them were *mean* drunks. Richard Burton, who was a sweet man when he was sober, was a horribly mean man when he was drunk and had to have a bodyguard to protect him from getting killed. It was the same with Bill Holden. He was a *very* nice guy, but when he got drunk, he was so damn nasty, he was just impossible. So was Tracy."

Another such alcoholic eruption was yet to come on *The Mountain,* but, in the interim, Dmytryk revelled in Tracy's artistry, his piquant gruffness and his wit.

Concerning Tracy's artistry, Dmytryk repeats what many others have said. About his sense of pace ("He didn't do pretentious things; there was no fat in his performance"); his unique ability to underplay ("He didn't *really* underplay. He just knew that, unlike a stage play, there are a lot of lines in a screenplay that are not important, and he correctly gave each line the importance it deserved"); his ability to pay attention to what the other actors were doing and saying, and reacting accordingly ("He *listened*. He wasn't just interested in his *own* next line, so he was able to conduct coherent, meaningful conversations that made sense. Jack Lemmon's the best actor today with that quality. Even if it's just a conversation with a bellboy, he *listens*, and remains believable").

Dmytryk adds that, like Montgomery Clift, Tracy was an actor who could give his very best performance in the first take made by him as a director, "unlike Marlon Brando, who wasn't any good until take seven." Dmytryk tells about one scene Tracy did in *The Mountain*, with E. G. Marshall, a pretty fair actor himself. Says Dmytryk, "We were in cramped quarters and when we got to the end of the scene, Marshall had tears in his eyes. So did half the crew. Marshall turned away and said, 'Goddamit, I wish all the method actors in the world could watch this man for just five minutes.' "

Concerning Tracy's crotchetiness, Dmytryk thinks back to an incident that occurred in his previous film with Tracy, *Broken Lance*. Says Dmytryk,

"To save money on location in Arizona, the studio had sent lime-filled pails for toilets. I said to Spence, 'You better be very careful when you sit on one of those pails. The lime might splash up there and burn your ass.' Spence said, 'I see what you mean,' and he called for his car. He told the production manager that he had to go to the john, so he was driving over to Ambassador Douglas's house, where he was staying, and which was twenty miles away. By the time he got back, the production manager, or somebody, had hauled up a proper vehicle with proper toilets in it, which we call a 'honey-wagon', and which required two extra drivers. No one was going to fool with Tracy when he got obstreperous, especially over such a minor thing as a toilet."

Another example of Tracy's acerbity. Says Dmytryk, "On *The Mountain,* young Bob Wagner was complaining about me. He said to Tracy, 'That Dmytryk really works the hell out of you. He made me do that goddam scene twice, at twelve thousand feet where I could hardly breathe.' Spence replied, 'Young man, you ought to get down on your hands and knees every night and thank God you work in the most overpaid business in the world.' "

Dmytryk soon learned that he could not overwork Tracy, even at lower altitudes, and used a mountain-guide double for him whenever he could. Dmytryk says, with considerable sadness,

"I couldn't believe how much Spence had aged in the couple of years since I had worked with him in *Broken Lance*. In that picture, I had to chide him by reminding him he had been a two-goal polo player, just to get him to ride a horse. But he did it. I don't know whether it was the booze, but his health had deteriorated so, by the time we did *The Mountain,* that I hesitated even to ask him to climb rocks.

"I'll never forget a very sad incident that happened when we first arrived in the Alps. We were at a comparatively low altitude and I started him out by taking walks with him. We went further and further each day, and finally he was very proud of himself when he got up a steep rise in the road in the woods. But then, along came a little old French woman, maybe ninety years old, about 4 feet 10 inches tall, carrying a metal, fifty-pound can of milk on her back. She scurried up the same rise in the road as if it were a flat cow-pasture down in the valley. Spence looked at her go chugging past, and I've never seen a man so deflated in my life. He got in the car, scowling, and never said a word all the way back to the hotel."

By judiciously conserving Tracy's strength, the filming went well for Dmytryk, except for Alcoholic Incident Number One, when the funicular cable car slipped its cog. Alcoholic Incident Number Two occurred when the filming in the Alps was completed, and the cast had to fly back to Hollywood to wind up production on a Paramount Studios sound stage. There is no hearsay in *this* description of a Tracy binge. Dmytryk, still an intense admirer, witnessed it all personally.

"The day we finished shooting in the Alps, the French mountain guides threw a party for us and we all were given honorary-guide badges. Some idiot gave Spence a glass of beer, and that's all it took to set him off. I think he was afraid again of that long airplane flight back home, but whatever it was, by the time we got into our cars for the ride of seventy kilometres or so to Geneva, he was drinking beer and throwing the empty bottles out of the window, at the rate of about two bottles per kilometer.

"In Geneva, we had about an hour's wait for the flight to Paris, and Spence switched to wine. In Paris, we had another wait of about eight hours for the plane to the United States, and, by now, Spence was on hard liquor. We finally got on the plane, and, halfway across, he was shouting at the stewardesses because they weren't bringing the booze fast enough. They told me that eventually he had drunk up everything on the plane. He was raising so much hell that they radioed ahead as we approached Los Angeles, and the aircraft pulled over to a remote part of the field to let him off. His wife and his daughter were waiting for him, and they carried him away with his brother, Carroll, who had been with us in Chamonix and was travelling with him.

"But that wasn't the end of the incident. Somehow, he got hold of Anna Kashfi, later Marlon Brando's wife, who was in our cast and who had gotten off the plane with us at the regular airline terminal. He dragged Anna around with him from bar to bar for several nights. Carroll Tracy also was with them and had to pay off a group of musicians whom Spence had hired for five thousand dollars to accompany them and to play for them at every night-spot that hit Spence's fancy. Carroll told me Spence didn't sleep at all, until he passed out for good. That didn't surprise me, because I knew all about his insomnia, which had gotten worse since he worked with me in *Broken Lance*. While he was doing *The Mountain,* I doubt that he slept more than two hours a night. Once, I caught him in the woods early in the morning, memorizing his lines, not for that day's shooting, but for a scene we weren't scheduled to do for another three days. So much for Spence's pretense that he never had to study his lines very much."

The upshot of the flying home from Chamonix incident was that Tracy once again disappeared for his customary two weeks. He was back to his old tricks. Kate was still away in Australia. He did not show up until production was well under way again at Paramount, with Dmytryk, in the meantime, using the mountain-guide Tracy-double he had wisely brought back with him from France. Says Dmytryk, "Tracy was fine when he at last arrived — no apologies, no explanations — and we finished the picture not too much over schedule. But the incident left me just as bitter about alcohol as I was when I promised myself I'd never work with Montgomery Clift again. Alcohol is worse than dope, and it's ruined more good people."

One might argue that Tracy's binges rarely hurt anyone else; that the only one he was ruining was himself. But what about the self-destruction of a great talent like Spencer Tracy, even when it was *done* by Spencer Tracy?

And what about the dual image of the man, as seen in the same picture by two different people, Robert Wagner and Edward Dmytryk?

Chapter Twenty-four

After *The Mountain,* working again with Kate in *Desk Set* was the usual exhilarating experience for Tracy, but it turned out to be one of the lesser of the Tracy-Hepburn pictures. The film was adapted from a stage play, and, although the scenario was done by the talented Phoebe and Henry Ephron, it was difficult to overcome the static quality of the stage-sound set and dialogue. The story was about an efficiency expert who comes into an office to establish what today would be called computerization. The expert (Tracy) runs foul of the office staff, headed by Hepburn, but also including Joan Blondell and Dina Merrill. Much of the old male-female sparring between Tracy and Hepburn was there, but perhaps it was diluted by the presence of two other formidable actresses and *their* witty lines which survived from the original stage play.

Perhaps, too, it was because Tracy was not feeling too well most of the time. The usual physical pattern with alcoholics is damage to the body's waste elimination systems (the liver and kidneys), which puts an additional strain on the heart and the lungs. In 1957, the year of *Desk Set,* Tracy began seeing a cardiologist regularly. He was also in low spirits because of the poor reception received by *The Mountain,* and, according to George Cukor, beginning to worry about his capabilities in selecting pictures for himself. Robert Wagner says, "He was the Marlon Brando of his time, a rebel against the studios," but he must have missed the discipline of the studios in finding vehicles for its stars, good or bad, but at least workable.

As a freelance, he had not done too well so far in choosing his film properties, but neither did Clark Gable when he left MGM, or Jack Lemmon, for a while, after his departure from Columbia. But when Leland Hayward and Warner Brothers came to Tracy with the Ernest Hemingway book *The Old Man and the Sea,* Tracy thought he had hit gold.

Six million dollars were sunk into the film. It was difficult to get much excitement into endless pictures of an old man in a boat in pursuit of a large fish, and, midway through the filming, the fine director, Fred Zinnemann, gave up, after constant arguments with Tracy and Hayward. Zinnemann was replaced by John Sturges, with whom Tracy had made *Bad Day at Black* Rock, among other good films. Yet, as the months went on, with money being spent on scenic background shots from as far away as Peru, Tracy grew more and more restive.

Then, there was a crisis which, as usual, was hushed up by the publicity department, this time Warner Brothers'. Columnist James Bacon was privy to the crisis. Says Bacon,

"I was playing golf with Ernie Borgnine at the Riviera Country Club one Saturday morning. We were on the fourth or fifth hole, when the starter came out in a golf cart. The starter said, 'Mr Borgnine, your agent called. He wants you to get back to him right away. It's very urgent.'

"Ernie went off in the golf cart and came back in about a half hour. He said, 'You won't believe this. Tracy and Hemingway got drunk and smashed up a Havana bar. The bar owner wants $150,000 to repair the damage and Jack Warner won't pay it. So Warner wants me to stand by at a moment's notice to go to Cuba and replace Tracy in *The Old Man and the Sea*.' Well, the upshot was that Warner did pay the damage, and Tracy did stay in the picture, but it sure caused a flap around the studio for a while."

Borgnine confirmed to me that the Jim Bacon account was correct; Warner Brothers had indeed called him on the golf course to stand by as a replacement for Tracy in *Old Man and the Sea*. Borgnine said,

> "The feeling I got was that they were afraid Mr. Tracy was going to blow up Havana, but even so, I kept saying to myself, 'They must be crazy. *Me* relieving Spencer Tracy?' Actually they must have been pretty serious because they also called in five other guys, but I was on top of the list. After a while, it all quieted down, and they told me I didn't have to stand by any more and could go back to playing golf. Kate was down there in Havana with Mr. Tracy and she evidently took care of the problem. I don't blame Mr. Tracy. He was so bored with that picture, it went on, and on, and on. And Christ, he had to get something out of his system, ya know."

After all this hassle, it is not surprising that the picture was an historic flop and Tracy got devastating reviews: "Papier-mâché performance"; "Tracy usually plays himself with a difference. This time he plays himself with indifference"; "Playing a Mexican peasant, he has not even taken the trouble to adapt his speech to the part"; "He sulked at the director and hardly bothered to act at all."

Apparently sensing this reaction in advance, Tracy rushed to do *The Last Hurrah* at Columbia with his old discoverer, director John Ford, even before *The Old Man and the Sea* went into release. Tracy told me, *"The Last Hurrah* was like aspirin to me after a very bad headache. It was just what I needed, the kind of story I'd done before and was comfortable with. And I had a lot of my old buddies in it—Pat O'Brien, Frank McHugh, Jimmy Gleason. It was like an alumni meeting of The Boys' Club from back in the 1930s."

The inclusion of Pat O'Brien in the cast was yet another example of the *good* side of the Jekyll/Hyde-like Tracy. His old friend, O'Brien, had fallen on hard times. "From 1950 to 1964," O'Brien wrote, "I made only three pictures." (It was more like eight.) Curiously, he blamed his downfall on the anti-Communist witch-hunt in Hollywood, which, in reverse, made him, a conservative, persona non grata among the left-wingers he claimed were still in power after the purges. More likely, the stereotypical Irishman he played had gone out of style.

Whatever the reason, Tracy's heart went out to his buddy from Milwaukee and the struggling days in New York. When he had starred in *The People Against O'Hara* at MGM, in 1951, Tracy had insisted that the second lead go to O'Brien, even to the point of threatening Dore Schary that he would walk out of the picture unless O'Brien got the part. O'Brien got the part.

The same thing happened when Tracy did The *Last Hurrah,* although it was an easier sell this time because John Ford, a fellow Irishman, liked O'Brien, too.

The picture was based on the Edwin O'Connor novel about the last campaign of a dying political boss in New England, reminiscent of the late Mayor James M. Curley of Boston. With Tracy, O'Brien and other Irishmen to work with, director John Ford derived a satisfactory amount of Celtic wit and cynicism from the cast, and the picture did well, both with the critics and at the box-office. Tracy got his first glowing reviews since *Bad Day at Black Rock,* with *Time Magazine* even suggesting he should win the Oscar for it. In one of the strange quirks of Academy Award balloting, Tracy *did* get an Oscar nomination for that year, 1958, but not for The Last Hurrah. It was for the critically despised *The Old Man and the Sea.*

Deeply wounded nevertheless, Tracy went into seclusion, seeing only Kate, his children, his doctors, and, from time to time, his wife Louise. Tracy unfailingly supported Louise financially, just as he had when they were living together, and she had now moved to a handsome house off Benedict Canyon, which rises into the low Santa Monica mountains above Beverly Hills. In speaking about his wife, he rarely referred to her as Louise, but nearly always as "the lady on the hill."

Settled into his own little retreat, down below on the George Cukor property, Tracy suffered through the entire year, 1959, during which there were no phone calls from the studios offering him work. Hepburn did not work in films, either, that year, after finishing *Suddenly Last Summer* at Columbia. Said George Cukor, "By now Kate was devoting herself almost entirely to taking care of Spence, and keeping him on the wagon." Tracy told me that in 1959 he was convinced he was through, that "nobody wanted me for a picture any more".

Quietly observing all this from the sidelines was producer director Stanley Kramer, himself considered a rebel in Hollywood for his socially aware pictures like *The Men* and *The Defiant Ones*.

Kramer had taken careful note of Tracy's struggles as a freelance actor, with *The Mountain* and *The Old Man and the Sea,* and he began to plan a course of action that would re-enrich the reputation of the ailing and ageing ex-superstar.

And in so doing, Kramer would also become the principal chronicler of the last days of the fascinating puzzle that was Spencer Tracy.

Chapter Twenty-five

Says Kramer sadly, "I was sort of the sunset of Tracy's life."

If so, what a magnificent sunset! Three Oscar nominations in four pictures. And while Tracy was literally a dying man.

Stanley Kramer never really knew Tracy until that day in 1960 when he sought him out in the hermitage to which he had retreated, the little rented house on George Cukor's property, from which he and Hepburn now rarely emerged. Kramer, thirteen years Tracy's junior, had been an assistant film director at MGM just after World War II, but Tracy, a superstar at MGM at the same time, had been just a dim, distant image to him. Says Kramer,

"All I knew about Spence was what everyone else at the studio knew. He was a raging bull. He used to get drunk and throw furniture through the plate glass windows of restaurants, tables and all. He'd disappear for two weeks at a time. The studio had an ambulance to go fetch him when he got into trouble. All the stuff you've heard about from other people. The important thing was that I studied his pictures in the cutting room. I recognized his greatness. I hoped he'd work with me some day when I grew up to become a film-maker."

Kramer grew up rather quickly. He soon became Hollywood's Boy Wonder as a producer. He teamed up with writer Carl Foreman and helped start the major trend toward hard-hitting melodramas based on contemporary social problems. He exposed racial injustices in *Home of the Brave,* he zeroed in on ill-treatment of paraplegic war veterans in *The Men,* he delved into the forces driving motorcycle gangs in *The Wild One.* These were the kinds of "message pictures" Louis B. Mayer loathed, but Kramer did not work for Mayer, or anyone else. He was one of the first of the true independents, and, contrary to the opinion of Mayer and others, his films made money—partially because Kramer had the knack of introducing dazzling new stars. Marlon Brando's first film, for example, was Kramer's *The Men;* his fifth was *The Wild One.* The eccentric but wily Howard Hughes was an early recognizer of Kramer's worth. Hughes offered Kramer the job of RKO studio-head when Kramer was only thirty-two years old. Kramer says, "I turned the job down because, as I told him, 'Let's not kid ourselves. *You'd* be running the studio not me.' So then the son of a bitch sued me for a six-minute scene in my film, *Champion,* which he claimed I had taken from some property he owned."

It was another ten years before Kramer finally brought Tracy into his life, the ambition he had harboured since his assistant-editor days at MGM. By then, Kramer (now also a director) had cemented his reputation as impresario of the offbeat, with such films as *The Pride and the Passion* (with the strange acting team of Cary Grant and Frank Sinatra); *The Defiant Ones* (with an equally amusing teaming of Tony Curtis and Sidney Poitier); and *On the Beach* (in which he shocked the movie world by casting dancer Fred Astaire in the straight dramatic role of a survivor of nuclear war).

Kramer, a student of history, had always been fascinated by the Scopes "monkey trial," in Tennessee in 1925, at which a young teacher was accused of violating a state law which prohibited the teaching of evolution, or any theory which conflicted with the Bible. The trial was a classic confrontation between the famous lawyer Clarence Darrow (on the side of evolution) and the silver-tongued ex-Presidential candidate William Jennings Bryan (on the side of the Bible). Kramer acquired a slightly fictionalized play about the trial, with the principal antagonists now named Drummond (for Darrow)

277

and Brady (for Bryan).

"From the very beginning," says Kramer, "I knew there was only one actor in the world to play the Clarence Darrow character—and that was Spencer Tracy. I called him and we had a meeting. He played it close to the vest, didn't give me too much warmth. He said, 'I might as well do it. Nobody else wants me. It would be better than just sitting home. But I'm ill. I don't have much energy.' I didn't know what was wrong with him, but I later found out it was the kidneys, bladder and liver. I said I would arrange the shooting schedule to tax him as little as possible and give him plenty of rest. He said OK, he'd do it.

"Spence perked up when I told him the people I had in mind for the rest of the casting. The William Jennings Bryan character was to be played by his old friend, Fredric March, and I had another of my offbeat ideas, to cast Gene Kelly in the straight dramatic role of a reporter, based on the great journalist, H. L. Mencken of the *Baltimore Sun*. That appealed to Spence and he said, 'Maybe we could have some fun on this picture.' "

And fun he *did* have, despite his continuing illness and constant feelings of weakness. But not before a potentially hazardous flap with Kramer, which occurred on the very first day of filming. Recalls Kramer (and this is an anecdote he relates every time the subject of Tracy comes up): "On that first day on the set, Spence destroyed me. We made a shot, and when I said 'Cut', the sound man came up to me and said, 'I didn't get the last part of that line because he kind of mumbled it off.' So I said, 'Spence, can we do another take?' He said, 'Why?' I said, 'Well, the sound man said we didn't get a little bit of that mumble at the end.' "

Kramer recites the rest of the incident with mounting drama.

"The whole crew is standing there, looking at me. And Tracy is looking at me. Do you know how long it is to look at somebody on a stage or in a film for ten seconds. Boy, it's an eternity. Tracy looked at me for ten seconds. Then he said, *Mister* Kramer.' Just like that. *Mister* Kramer,' he said, 'It has taken me just about forty years to learn to read a line that way. Now do you want some college kid from UCLA to come over here and do this? Just say so, and we can arrange it.' You know, that's some put-down for a director. But I looked at him for a minute, and I calmly said, 'Well, OK Spence, can we do another take?' He said, 'OK, let's do another take.' "

The crisis was over, and, from that moment on,

Tracy and Kramer became the closest of friends. Was he testing this director, with whom he never had worked before? Probably. Did Kramer pass the Tracy test? Probably, because he did not back down. Kramer believes this was Tracy's way of letting him know, from day one, that he would not stand for a lot of takes, that he was too ill and tired to do so, but that he soon found "that I understood, that I had patience, that I had some talents which evidently fit some grooves with him."
Adds Kramer,

"After that touchy beginning, I don't think we ever had a cross word in the seven years I knew him. I got to love him as a human being, and I think he loved me, but Spence's idea of loving was to play the curmudgeon, which is what he did constantly with Kate Hepburn. I could never tell him he was a wonderful actor, because he'd get embarrassed and say something like, 'Shit, what kind of fuckin' gag is that? I'm just doing my job.' Yet, later, when I said in a press conference in Paris that Oskar Werner was as great an actor as one would want to work with, Spence sent me a clipping of my quote in the *New York Herald-Tribune*. He had written in red pencil on the clipping, 'What the hell is this?' I sent Spence a cable, saying, 'What you don't understand about that quote is that I was speaking only of mortal actors.' "

Once they had established their ground rules, filming was indeed fun for both Tracy and Kramer on *Inherit the Wind*. It was also a special event for the entire film industry. It was almost like a hit stage play, with people battling for the privilege to get in to watch the action. Says Kramer,

"We had Tracy and Fredric March nose to nose for long courtroom confrontations and assorted histrionics. The sound stage was filled with celebrities and executives from every studio in town. And how Tracy and March luxuriated in the applause of this audience. Every take brought down the house, and their escapades were something to see. They teased and goaded each other with every trick they had learned over the years. It all showed up on the screen. For example, everyone who saw the picture will remember how Freddie would fan himself vigorously with a large undertaker's fan each time Spence would launch into an oration. And then how Spence would cause a distraction by pulling at his nose, especially during March's three and a half minute summation to the jury."

One trick of Tracy's, which never failed to bring the house down with the sound-stage audience, was his uncanny ability to use the ten-second pause for intense dramatic effect.

"When he did that," says Kramer, "you could literally see the wheels go around in his head every time the camera was turned on him. I remember one magnificent example. He had March on the witness stand and he said, 'So all of these, all of these biological results, were brought about through the common ordinary thing we call sex.' That's the way the lines were written, but it's what Tracy did with them. There was that ten-second pause, during which you could *see* him thinking, and he said with apparent cunning, 'What do you think of sex, Mr Brady?' Just like that. The cast and crew, the onlookers in the sound stage, gave him a standing ovation before I could even film March's response. It was one of the highlights of the picture."

Kate Hepburn was nearly always in the audience. "She wasn't working," says Kramer. "She was spending all her time looking after Spence, arriving with him in the morning, making sure he took his medicines and drank his milk, leaving with him when he was through in the afternoon. She was like a nurse-companion to him." Kramer paused thoughtfully and added, "Or a wife."

Kramer was one of the very few people Tracy and

Hepburn invited over to the little rented house on the Cukor property.

"I'd go there for dinner, sometimes, after the day's shooting, and Kate would do all the cooking. Funny, but I remember she always made the same dessert, hot chocolate fudge sundaes. Spence generally was quiet and I couldn't help notice the gradual deterioration of his health, but he still had those same spirited verbal exchanges with Kate, which always reminded me of the characters they played in *Woman of the Year.* Kate would venture one of her strong opinions about Russian missiles, for example, and Spence would sneer at her, 'So that's another one of those subjects you know all about.' Instead of blowing her top, like she would with anyone else, Kate would just giggle and say, 'Oh, Spencuh,' just like that. And Spence would come back with that line I mentioned before: 'Why do you always talk like you've got a feather up your ass?'

"What a strange, wonderful relationship. In my opinion, by tolerating his cantankerousness, Kate was allowing him to play a part which best suited his defense mechanisms. On the other hand, he allowed her to fuss over him, where, you know, it would bother him if anyone else did it. And the loving and respect that came through! I'd discuss a suggested change with him on the set and he'd say, 'Let me see what Kate thinks.' And she'd come over to me on the set, time and time again, and say, 'Boy, he's really something, isn't he?' And I thought *she* was really something, so all in all, it was quite remarkable, because this is a very independent woman.'

The loving and the sparring went on through the rest of the filming of *Inherit the Wind,* and then Tracy and Hepburn retreated again to the seclusion of the little house on St. Ives. Kramer continued to see them, but only occasionally. Kramer says, "Spence paid me the greatest compliment. One night he said, 'Stanley, any picture you want to do with me, I want to do it with you.'"

Then came the usual waiting period for the picture to be seen by the public. In the case of *Inherit the Wind,* Tracy did not have to wait too long. The film was released late in 1960, the year in which it was made. The Academy Award nominations were announced a couple of months later.

Tracy had won his *seventh* Oscar nomination as Best Actor, for the role of Henry Drummond in *Inherit the Wind.*

Chapter Twenty-six

The chance for Tracy to work again with Kramer came sooner than anyone expected. It also came in a circuitous way.

It was the so-called Golden Age of Television, and writer Abby Mann had written a remarkable drama for *Playhouse 90*. It was called *Judgment at Nuremberg,* and Mann had based it on the war-crimes trials conducted in Germany by the victorious Allies after World War II. The television play starred Claude Rains, Maximilian Schell, Paul Lukas and Melvyn Douglas. The show won multiple Emmys and was quite a triumph for Mann, who was in his early twenties when he first started writing the project. He had tried to sell an expanded version of the TV drama as a movie, but that was a period of great timidity in the film industry. Everyone was apprehensive about a film that touched on the slaughter of six million Jews in the Nazi concentration camps. So no movie deal. Every studio passed.

Mann told me:

"I had pretty much given up on getting the movie done, and I was now concentrating on converting it into a play for Broadway. In fact, the Theater Guild had taken an option on the property. But I was in Europe, trying to talk Ingrid Bergman into doing *A Child is Waiting,* another successful teleplay I had written, the first about the problems of mentally retarded children. Along the way, I stopped off to see the British director, Jack Clayton, who had scored a big movie hit with *Room at the Top.* Clayton was interested in doing *A Child is Waiting,* but, to my amazement, he was more interested in *Judgment at Nuremberg* as a movie. He had seen a kinescope of the TV version and thought it would make one helluva film.

"Clayton said to me, 'Is there any way I could get you to drop the idea of doing it as a play and making it as a film, instead?' Reminding him that all the American movie studios had passed on it, I said, 'The only way I would consider it as a film would be if you got Spencer Tracy to play the Claude Rains role.' He said, 'OK,' and I forgot about it and went back to pursuing Ingrid Bergman.

"The next thing I knew, I got a phone call from my agent, telling me that Stanley Kramer wanted to do *Judgment at Nuremberg* with Spencer Tracy. I didn't find out until later how this strange turn of events came about. Jack Clayton and Tracy had the same agents, William Morris. The agents told Tracy about Clayton's interest in doing the movie, but said the director wanted to shoot it only in the authentic locale, Germany. Tracy then went to Kramer. He told Kramer, 'I think this is an important picture, but I can't go to Europe. I'm too sick. I want to do the movie here, with *you.*'

I must say I shouldn't have been surprised because Tracy loved Stanley, admired his talents, and felt very comfortable with him after *Inherit the Wind.* But anyway, after that phone call from my agent, I flew back to New York and met with Stanley at the Plaza Hotel, and we had a deal, with my idol, Spencer Tracy, already having agreed to star in the film. Spence had been my idol ever since the first play I had ever seen in my life, *The Rugged Path,* when I was a young kid in New York and watched him from the top of the second balcony."

Ironic, when you remember how Tracy hated the play and did everything he could to get out of it.

Also ironic: here was a supposedly apolitical Tracy caring enough about the tragedy of the Jews in the Nazi Holocaust to defy all Hollywood wisdom in even wanting to make the film. A third irony: Tracy, who had feuded with producers all his life, now only wanted to be reunited with Stanley Kramer in a film venture that could be extremely difficult for a sick and tired old man (although he was still only sixty-one).

Once again, when filming began, Kramer made special provisions in his shooting schedule to give Tracy all the rest he needed. Actually, the role was nowhere near as tiring as the two-man *tour de force* he had staged with Fredric March. In *Judgment at Nuremberg,* he played a retired judge from Maine, who presided at the war-crimes trial of four former Nazi judges, one of whom, for some reason known only to Kramer, was played by Burt Lancaster. The meatiest role in the film was that of the German defence counsel, Hans Rolfe, played by Maximilian Schell in a reprise of the same role in which he had sparkled in Abby Mann's *Playhouse 90* version. The wily Tracy recognized the fact that Schell's role dominated the screenplay, and also that the nearly unknown Schell was an actor of enormous talent. On the very first day of filming, Tracy was chattering with Richard Widmark, his friend from *Broken Lance.* Both were watching out of the corners of their eyes while Schell did a scene. Widmark, who played the US prosecutor opposite Schell's defence attorney, later told me, "Spence kept looking at Max at work on the sound stage, and then he turned to me and said, 'We've got to watch out for that young man. He's very good. He's going to walk away with the Oscar for this picture.'"

Tracy's own role, the simple down-to-earth judge from New England, was made to order for him. He was playing the common man again, and he was enjoying himself.

"Nonetheless," says Kramer, "the cranky curmudgeon continued to come through once in a while. For example, there was a flap on the set involving a pastrami sandwich. Yes, a pastrami sandwich. It was being eaten, between takes, by a fairly well-known actor—I won't embarrass him by naming him—who was playing one of the American judges. I once wrote that Tracy threatened to murder this actor, and perhaps that was an exaggeration. But Spence did fly into a rage, probably because it was destroying everyone's concentration. He yelled at the guy, 'How the hell can we be passing judgement on four guys, imprisoning them for life for war crimes beyond comprehension, and, knowing all that, how the hell can you munch on that sandwich?'

"In retrospect it was funny. But that was Spence. He was taking the picture very seriously, mostly because of one line that pumped him up—about the value of a single human life, let alone the millions who were slaughtered in the Holocaust—and he wanted everyone else to take the picture very seriously, too."

Abby Mann recalls an incident when he was sitting with Marlene Dietrich,

"and Tracy was storming up and down and giving me dirty looks." Says Mann, "I went over and asked him, 'What's the matter?' and he said, 'Don't you know she has Billy Wilder re-writing all your lines?' So the next time, when Marlene came in with her script with 'little changes' in it, I tore up the script and she had to go out and read my lines as written. Then Tracy got mad at me because he thought I had gone too far with Marlene. But he'd go on the set and call the whole cast together, and he'd say, 'The script this man has worked on is the best damned script we've ever had, and I don't want any changes. And that goes for this guy, n' this guy, n' this guy, n' this guy,' pointing at Schell, Lancaster, all the big stars. It was hard to figure Spence out sometimes."

More dichotomy:

"As ill as Spence was," says Kramer, "his heart went out to Judy Garland and Montgomery Clift, who were both in the last stages of the same disease he had. Monty was ill, very ill, because of the booze and the drugs, and it was Spence who pulled him through. Monty couldn't remember his lines. He could barely remember his own name. Yet he was on the stand, playing a guy who had been sterilized, and, when you look at the film now, it was a magnificent performance. How did Spence do it? He grabbed Monty by the shoulders and told him he was the greatest young actor alive. Then he said to Monty, 'Look, it doesn't matter to Stanley, or to me, what the words are. Stop trying to remember the lines and just look into my eyes and tell me how you feel.' And Monty did that. He took a picture out of his pocket and said, 'My, my mother, you know.' And he winged the whole scene, looking into Spence's eyes. I think that saved Monty's life for a little longer because he got an Academy nomination, and he was proud of it."

So here was Tracy, the big believer in preparation, bending the rules out of compassion for another human being. And yet the other Tracy, the martinet in the matter of an actor being ready, was also evident in this same film. Says Kramer,

"I had a guy who was playing a small part. He had to come in a room and wait for Tracy to make an entrance, and give him a folder or something. Well, this guy was a young actor out of New York, and he was hung up on motivation. What is my motivation to come into the room and walk over to the table? I was trying to go along with him so that he could gratify himself or satisfy himself, either one.

"Tracy finally came out of his dressing room, because he had been sitting there since nine in the morning and it was now ten fifteen. 'Lookit,' he said to the young actor, and these are his exact words: 'You come in the fuckin' door, and cross the fuckin' room, and go to the fuckin' table, because it's the only way to get in the fuckin' room. That's your motivation.' "

More dichotomy: Kramer told me, as had Gene Kelly and others, "I don't really feel that Spence had any politics. To my knowledge, he never campaigned for anybody for President, or supported any cause in terms of being an activist. I, myself, was heavily influenced in my youth by the first Roosevelt years, but this was beyond Spence's interest cycle." On the other hand, Abby Mann comes up with the startling news that not only was Franklin D. Roosevelt very *much* in Tracy's interest cycle, but that Tracy actually *knew* the New Deal President personally.

Says Mann:

"Like Eddie Dmytryk, I never subscribed to the view that Spence was apolitical. The writer Dalton Trumbo told me that when he was blacklisted and shunned by everyone in Hollywood, Tracy made a point of coming over to his table one night in Romanoff's restaurant and speaking to him loudly and amiably, in a way that everyone could hear. But even so, I was surprised by what happened one day on the set of *Judgment at Nuremberg*.

"What happened," continued Mann, "was that Supreme Court Justice William O. Douglas showed up on the set. I had no idea that Tracy knew him, and I brought the Justice over to meet our star. Spence, who liked to needle me, said, 'Take your Communist friends and go to hell.' I was terribly embarrassed until we ran into Douglas again at lunch in the commissary, and Tracy and Douglas threw their arms around each other. Then I began to get the picture. But as we three ate lunch together, I got more and more swept away. At one point, Tracy said to me, 'You know, this son-of-a-bitch could have been President of the United States, but the bastard didn't want it.' "

Mann's next question, naturally, was "How?" and Tracy startled him by talking casually about a lunch he had had one day with President Roosevelt. "With

Roosevelt?" said Mann.

"Yeah," said Tracy, "Bill was there."

Justice Douglas nodded concurrence. As Mann goes on with the story, Tracy said, "At this lunch I had with the President, Mr. Roosevelt says, pointing at Douglas, 'I wanted this son of a bitch to run for Vice President instead of Harry Truman, but he wouldn't give up girls,' and Bill here says, 'It ain't worth it.' " The astounded Abby Mann then listened to Tracy say, "So this man would have been President, instead of that haberdasher." Mann struggled to ask Justice Douglas if all this actually had taken place in the White House between Roosevelt, Tracy and himself. Mann says, "Douglas answered, 'You're damned right.' "

On the whole, with visits from VIPs like Douglas, Tracy, despite his weakened condition, had quite a stimulating experience doing *Judgment at Nuremberg.* Again, Kate Hepburn was at his side throughout the production. Also, the set at Universal Pictures was clogged with a repeat of the studio celebrities and executives flocking to watch him work in his key courtroom scenes. There was a near mob-scene when he broke his own endurance record for a single speech in a movie. That was a record thirteen minutes and forty-two seconds for his final summation at the end of the Nazi judges' trial, using some of the real words of the real Justice Robert Jackson at Nuremberg: "This is what we stand for . . . justice . . . truth . . . and the value of a single human being."

Yet, with all the encomium, all the excitement, there was another example of the conflicts that raged within Tracy. Says Abby Mann, "When he wasn't on camera, he'd get in his Thunderbird and ride back and forth, back and forth, past all the sets and sound stages at Universal Studios. Then he'd come over to me and ask, 'Are we all right?' It was that terrible insecurity of his. He had to be reassured constantly that his performance, and the film itself, were doing well."

When production ended, Tracy felt slightly better about the picture because of the publicity generated by his closing scenes. But he was desperately weary. Kramer says, "I had scheduled the world premiere of the picture for West Berlin, and there was a question as to whether Spence would go or not. Kate didn't want him to go. She said he wasn't well, and that the situation in Germany was such that the premiere there was a political hot potato which might aggravate him and worsen his condition. But Spence said, 'Hey, come on, the man wants me to go, and I want to go.' So they *both* ended up making the trip to Berlin."

It was a political hot potato indeed. Germany was just being welcomed back into the family of nations, and nobody wanted to open up old wounds. Many Germans still did not believe that the Holocaust had even existed. There were many ex-Nazis who complained that Kramer, a Jew, was just trying to stir up trouble. Here he was with previously unseen authentic footage of concentration camp atrocities, which somehow he had smuggled out of the US Army Signal Corps files. And in his entourage was Marlene Dietrich, still considered a traitor among some Germans because she had entertained Allied troops during the war. The American diplomatic corps looked askance at Kramer's premiere. They did not want trouble with Adenauer's post-war Reich. Even Jews were saying, "The more you remind them of it, the more anti-Semitism there is."

The premiere went well, notwithstanding. The Germans in the audience were totally silent and thoughtful when the picture ended. There was only one untoward event, and it involved Tracy. Abby Mann says,

"I was there, and what happened was very disturbing. Monty Clift showed up at the premiere, stoned and drunk out of his mind. I was walking along with Spence and Dick Widmark, when we suddenly heard someone yell, 'Yippee!', and there was Monty, coming up from behind and jumping on Spence's back. Inside the theater, Monty became impossible. He was really freaking out, crawling on his hands and knees between the aisles. He went past my feet and everyone else's in our box, screaming out all sorts of crazy things. I looked at Spence and he was very upset. About half an hour into the picture, with Monty still carrying on, Spence got up and left. It crossed my mind that seeing Clift in that advanced state of deterioration might have reminded Spence of his own drinking problem."

The newspapers the next day reported that Tracy had left because of a flare-up of his kidney ailment, and he was not expected to show up at the press conference staged by Kramer at a restaurant called The Pregnant Oyster. But he did. And he masterfully handled questions from the hostile German press. Mann vividly remembers Tracy's sharp response to one key question. Says Mann, "A guy asked him, 'Do you really believe what was portrayed in this picture?' and Spence shot back with, 'Every word.' "

Later, Tracy was to receive his eighth Academy Award nomination for *Judgment at Nuremberg* but, as he had predicted, Maximilian Schell won the Oscar itself.

Earlier, on his way back from Berlin, Tracy, a prodigious telegram writer, sent a wire to Mann, who still has it hanging on the wall of his study at home.

The telegram reads, in part: "It was a great privilege to say those words [you wrote]. All I can say is if the lights go out now, I still win."

Chapter Twenty-seven

As his frailty gradually increased after *Judgment at Nuremberg,* Tracy apparently had more and more intimations of his own mortality, and he returned to the obsessions of his youth. His interest in the Catholic Church revived, and, said George Cukor, "Spence was reading a lot of books on Catholic theology in his little house. I remember I heard him playing a recording of Brahms' *Shicksalslied* one day and I went down to chat. He and Kate were listening to the music. Both were reading. Kate's book was a collection of Eugene O'Neill's plays. Spence's book was a well-worn copy of what he said was *All Things in Christ,* about a Pope Pius X, who had died in 1914 and later was made a saint, I think. Kate just looked up and said, 'Snappy reading.' "

In this period, too, Tracy renewed his acquaintanceship with Monsignor John O'Donnell, who, as a young priest, had been the technical adviser on Tracy's film, *Boys Town.*

One can't say for certain whether these factors had influenced Tracy to do a truly bad film, *The Devil at Four O'Clock,* in the short interval between *Inherit the Wind* and *Judgment at Nuremberg*, but Pat O'Brien speculated that "maybe Spence wanted to play a priest for one last time." In this case, interestingly enough, his role of Father Doonon was that of a *drunken* priest. As it turned out, the production was not a satisfying one for Tracy. He liked working with his co-star, Frank Sinatra, with whom he had been friends since both had regularly visited the dying Humphrey Bogart, and the friendship continued afterwards, with Tracy even attending the Sinatra-Mia Farrow wedding at a time when he never left the seclusion of his St. Ives retreat. But Sinatra liked to begin work at one o'clock in the afternoon, by which time Tracy, who had been on the set since early morning, was already fatigued. And then there was the previously mentioned matter of Tracy's playing to a broomstick in Sinatra's off-camera scenes. In any event, this final priest role for Tracy did not compare with Father Mullin in *San Francisco* and Father Flanagan in *Boys Town,* and the experience had left him temporarily disconsolate until he was perked up again by *Judgment at Nuremberg.*

By now it was 1962 and Kate Hepburn, in her self-imposed role of caring for the ailing Tracy, had not worked for three years. According to Abby Mann, who visited them from time to time, Kate tried to stimulate Tracy by interesting him in doing a significant project, like Ibsen's *The Master Builder*, in which, says Mann, "Spence would have been magnificent as an older architect, a made-to-order part for him.' " But, in his gruff way, Tracy always said, "Nah." Later in 1962, a significant project *did* come along for Hepburn, one in which Mann felt Tracy also would be magnificent. The project was Embassy Pictures' film version of Eugene O'Neill's *Long Day's Journey Into Night*.

Mann rushed up to see Tracy. Says Mann, "I told him, 'Spence, you've done tremendous roles, but that role, with you and Kate, you were just born to do it.' Spence said, 'Nah. I'm not going to do it.' I said, 'Why? It's a great play and you'll have a fine director, Sidney Lumet.' He said, 'I just would like to watch a picture with Kate in it — without me.' That was sad, really sad."

Hepburn ended up making *Long Day's Journey Into Night* with Ralph Richardson and Jason Robards, and it turned out to be an exceptional film. But not as exceptional as it would have been with Tracy. Why did he keep refusing the classics? As Angela Lansbury said, "He was best at playing the common man," and his previous ventures into the classics had been disasters: Robert Louis Stevenson's *Dr. Jekyll and Mr. Hyde,* John Steinbeck's *Tortilla Flat,* and Hemingway's *The Old Man and the Sea.*

301

He did not even feel comfortable in his Oscar-winner, Rudyard Kipling's *Captains Courageous*. So perhaps he was *afraid* to tackle anything, especially in his advanced frail state, that could even remotely be called a classic. If so, as Abby Mann said, "That was sad, really sad."

Sad, too, was another problem then besetting Tracy, which Mann had noticed. It was a worry common to many alcoholics in the latter stages of their disease. Says Mann, "Spence always had prided himself in his remarkable ability to learn and memorize lines, and now he had a constant fear of that memory-capacity deteriorating. On *Judgment at Nuremberg*, he'd keep sidling up to me and asking, 'Did Stanley say I couldn't remember my lines?' and he'd keep putting the same question to Kramer directly. The prospect of losing his memory was terrifying him." This may account for how unreasonably upset he got with Montgomery Clift at the *Judgment at Nuremberg* premiere, perhaps remembering how he had helped Clift through his memory loss during production.

So Tracy, with his fragile ego, seems to have been focusing on such fears, together with his early guilt about not having become a priest as his father had wished. This was during the period when Kate Hepburn was filming *Long Day's Journey Into Night*, and it may be significant that when she finished the picture, she did not do another for five more years. Even more than before, Tracy became her sole and overwhelming concern. Stanley Kramer certainly thought so.

It was Kramer who once again pulled Tracy out of the doldrums, late in 1962. Kramer, with the critical success of *Judgment at Nuremberg* behind him, decided he wanted to do a comedy. Why? Kramer says,

"It was simply a matter of ego, to tell you the truth. I had never done a comedy before, and I thought I could come up with a successful one, if it was filled with action, and tongue-in-cheek satire, and I could use a bunch of big-name comedians who would all play heavies. I also thought of Tracy, who hadn't done comedy in years. If you think about it, he was a natural for the role of an old police captain, with a haggling, niggling wife, to be played by Selma Diamond, and who chases all these comedians playing crooks, and finally ends up as an old crook himself who wants to run off with the money."

And so, *It's a Mad, Mad, Mad, Mad World* came into being, with a cast consisting of Milton Berle, Sid Caesar, Buddy Hackett, Ethel Merman, Mickey Rooney, Dick Shawn, Phil Silvers, Jonathan Winters, Terry-Thomas, Edie Adams and Jimmy Durante, among others, and with Spencer Tracy starring above them all, as the henpecked, old master of skullduggery, Captain C. G. Culpeper.

As Kramer puts it, "Spence really had a ball on this picture." For one thing, he did not have to work very hard. He was photographed mostly in close-up, while a double did all the running and stair-climbing for him. Secondly, this was the kind of slapstick he did when he was a George M. Cohan protégé in the theatre in the 1920s. And thirdly, all the brilliant comics were in awe of him, just as Ernest Borgnine had been in *Bad Day at Black Rock*.

Sid Caesar, for example, tells the extent to which *he* was in awe of Tracy. Says Caesar,

"It was early in the picture and I hadn't met Mr. Tracy yet. I was having a big fight with the writer, William Rose, over some lines of mine that I wanted to change. I was screaming and yelling. Stanley Kramer was there, and he got scared over my screaming and yelling. He ran out and came back with Mr. Tracy. The minute I saw this legend, I forgot all about my fight with Rose. I just shut up, didn't say another word. I guess that's why Stanley brought him in.

"Then I went into the Universal commissary and had lunch with Mr. Tracy. He started talking about the death of Marilyn Monroe, which had just happened, and about how much was disappearing from the old Hollywood. I was so tongue-tied, I couldn't say anything. When the waiter came over to take our order, I mumbled, 'I'll have what *he* has.' Mr. Tracy ordered soft-boiled eggs. Now, ordinarily I have a very big appetite, and soft-boiled eggs weren't enough for me. But if he had ordered soft-boiled shoes, I would have eaten soft-boiled shoes."

Kramer says,

"A lot of the picture was made in Palm Springs in the summer. It was very hot. So I had this big airconditioned truck, and, inside, it was lined with benches and stools and chairs. The cast all stayed there when they wanted to get away from the heat, and the comedians always were on, of course. Everybody played to Tracy. Everybody made jokes for his benefit, and he was laughing all the time, which was very good for him, you know. Buddy Hackett and Mickey Rooney improvised skits, with Hackett playing Father Flanagan and Rooney playing the bad boy. Hackett would say, in his way, 'Lookit now, who do you think you are, young fellow? You're going to learn some rules here.' And Rooney would say, 'Fuck you, you old bastard.'

"And Jonathan Winters would improvise entire Tracy-Hepburn movies, with Johnny playing both parts, along with all the sound effects. As Hepburn, he'd say, 'Who the hell are you?' and as Tracy, he'd say, 'I'm a sports writer, and I'd like to play with you, baby.' Like that. A lot of it was very dirty, and the guys kept breaking Tracy up."

Tracy predicted that the silly, little, offbeat film would gross a lot of money at the box-office. And it did. Twenty-odd years later, it is considered a cult film which still plays to overflow houses.

As for Kramer, he still feels good about the fact that doing the film made Tracy feel good. "I guess I automatically thought of him — what can I use Tracy for? Why should someone so great just be languishing around? And when I asked him to do *Mad, Mad World,* he simply said, 'You want me? Fine.' That made me feel good."

Concerning the state of Tracy's health while making the film, Kramer says, "He was weaker, but not as weak as he seemed to be on *Inherit the Wind.* As usual, I gave him short hours, to conserve his strength. As usual, too, I looked to see if he was drinking, but I never saw him take a drink on this picture, or on any of the other pictures he did for me. He always had a glass of milk with ice cubes in it.

"Of course, you might say, 'Maybe there was brandy in the milk.'

"But I wouldn't know."

Chapter Twenty-eight

In 1963, long before the release of *It's a Mad, Mad, Mad, Mad World*, Tracy went on his last known major boozing bender. This was the occasion when columnist James Bacon had to drive him, in an unconscious state, from Romanoff's restaurant in Beverly Hills to the beach house in Trancas, and when Katharine Hepburn said to Bacon, "God damn you, you've always been an evil companion for Spence."

The Trancas house had been rented from publicity executive Frank McFadden, and apparently had been planned by Hepburn to give Tracy some rest and relaxation for the summer, away from the cramped little St. Ives house in town.

On 21 July 1963, Tracy and Hepburn were about to embark on a Sunday picnic from the Trancas house. Suddenly, Tracy collapsed on the front seat of his car. He had trouble breathing and was suffering severe chest pains. Terribly alarmed, Kate called the Los Angeles County Fire Department for help from the paramedics. The Fire Department later said she had reported that Tracy had suffered an apparent heart attack.

The Fire Department's Captain Robert Robb told the Associated Press that when his resuscitator unit arrived, Tracy was still slumped in his car and that "he looked very pale and his breathing was labored." The rescue unit gave Tracy oxygen for forty-five minutes, and then he was taken by ambulance to St. Vincent's Hospital, with Hepburn riding along. At the hospital, Tracy's own physician, Dr. Karl Lewis, took charge, and subsequently announced to a swarm of reporters that Tracy had *not* suffered a heart attack and that the problem was a "congestive lung condition." In other words, his lungs had filled with fluid. No reason for the condition was given.

Tracy was in the hospital for two weeks. After that, it took him more than a year to recover fully. He spent all this time in the St. Ives house. Frank McFadden told me "they never returned to the Trancas house, though Hepburn had taken a lease on it for a minimum of six months."

Late in 1963, Tracy was offered a role in John Ford's western, *Cheyenne Autumn.* He became excited about being reunited with Ford, but, in December 1963, he had to announce that he was still too ill to take on the assignment. Edward G. Robinson got the role. In 1964, Tracy became even more excited when MGM spoke to him about doing *The Cincinnati Kid* with Steve McQueen. This was to be the story of an old poker player facing a challenge from a rising *young* poker player, and Tracy felt that the role of the old poker player was one of the those made-to-order parts for him. But once again his doctors said that he was still too ill from his now nearly two-year-old bout of "lung congestion," and he could not yet go back to work. And, strangely enough, it was Edward G. Robinson who once again replaced him.

Later that year, Stanley Kramer bought Katherine Anne Porter's best-selling novel, *Ship of Fools,* and he hired Abby Mann to write the screenplay. Kramer and Mann had been among the few people allowed to visit Tracy who, according to the Associated Press, was now also telling friends "that he had been having trouble with diabetes and had sores on his heels." Mann says that he and Kramer desperately wanted Kate Hepburn for the role eventually played by Vivien Leigh in *Ship of Fools,* but they had their eye on Oskar Werner for the key part of the doctor. Says Mann, "I had seen Werner do *Hamlet* in Germany, and we also thought he had been just wonderful in Anatole Litvak's picture *Decision Before Dawn*. He seemed perfect to play our doctor. Though we wanted Kate, we never considered Spence as the doctor."

All this led to an unhappy interlude one night at

the St. Ives house. Mann recalls,

"Stanley and I were invited up for dinner. Kate said she was going to cook steaks, which she had bought at Jurgensen's, one of the fine food stores in Beverly Hills. We arrived and were chatting about *Ship of Fools*. Stanley indicated how much he would like to have Kate in the film. Then Kate brought up the subject of Spence as the doctor. It was an awkward moment. Stanley's a very nice guy and began fishing around to get out of it some way. He finally said, 'Well, we've decided to go young with that part.' Kate said, 'I think I'll just throw the steaks from Jurgensen's in the garbage can.' We *did* eat the steaks, but the subject of *Ship of Fools* never came up again. We felt just awful. It was terribly, terribly sad, and Stanley told me he didn't sleep all that night, just thinking about Spence. And Kate did *not* do the picture."

But again, the strange dichotomy of Spencer Tracy emerged. Kramer says,

"As soon as we began filming on *Ship of Fools,* Spence asked me if he could just hang around the set and watch. I said, 'I'd be honored', and he was there nearly every day. So was Kate. They wanted to do everything they could to help and support Vivien Leigh, who was in very bad shape. Vivien had been married to Larry Olivier, their very good friend. And now, after the divorce, and Larry's marriage to Joan Plowright, she was falling apart. Like Monty Clift on *Judgment at Nuremberg,* she couldn't remember her lines. A couple of times she had to have electro-shock treatments to try to rearrange her brain cells. Spence worked patiently with Vivien, just as he'd done with Monty, and with his compassion for her, he was a big help to me."

Tracy, despite his own fears of loss of memory and despite his hurt at not being in the picture, was also a big help to Kramer in other ways. Kramer says,

"I learned a lot of things from Spence, especially about the pithy pause, which he did so well. I used it in one of the funniest scenes in *Ship of Fools,* a drunken dialogue between Lee Marvin and a dwarf. In fact, I used it three times in that short scene, and it's amazing how the laughter builds and builds in the pauses when an audience sees it in a theater. Spence was standing beside me when I shot that scene. I was just advancing what *he* did so effectively and I told him so. He said, kiddingly, 'Just see that I get the proper screen credit, buddy.' "

Members of the press witnessed the closeness of Kramer and Tracy behind the camera, and the rumour spread that Tracy was now planning to switch careers from acting to directing.

No such thing. Tracy said, "I wouldn't have the patience." He told Bob Thomas, "I was just hanging around because I got free lunch every day." When production finished, he dropped out of sight again in the little house on St. Ives. But only for a short time. On 30 August 1965, the news media were again in a hospital, this time Good Samaritan, covering another Tracy medical crisis.

It did not seem to be much of a crisis at first. Tracy was taken to Good Samaritan for tests and eventually for removal of part of his prostate gland, a fairly common procedure for a man of sixty-five. The surgery went well and it was announced that there was no evidence of cancer. But no surgery can be routine when a patient has kidneys and other organs ravaged by many years of alcohol abuse. It was never specifically stated, of course, that this was the case with Tracy. However, on 13 September (nine days after the operation, by which time most other patients would have been home), Tracy developed complications and was put on the hospital's critical list. A spokesman said that Tracy had developed "an electrolyte imbalance." This is a life-threatening situation, sometimes caused by haemorrhage and sometimes by ill-functioning kidneys, heart and lungs.

Tracy was taken off the critical list in twenty-four hours, but an internal Associated Press advisory stated that "a brother, Carroll Tracy, may be at the bedside when he dies." Also, the hospital asked a priest to be on call. Tracy gradually recovered, but he had to remain in the hospital for six weeks after his relatively minor operation. In another illustration of the anomaly of Tracy's life, Louise Tracy was a constant visitor at his hospital bedside; so was Kate Hepburn. But never at the same time.

George Cukor said, "Louise and Kate got together and worked out the schedule between them."

Chapter Twenty-nine

When he got home from Good Samaritan Hospital, there was another long period of enforced rest for Tracy. He was driven occasionally to see Louise, "the lady on the hill," and he spent as much time as he could with his children and with Monsignor O'Donnell. But mostly he read and listened to music with Kate. To the extent that his frailty allowed, she took long, slow walks with him. He remembered the fun he had had flying kites when he was a boy in Milwaukee, and when he felt well enough, Kate would drive him to some uncongested beach, and they would fly kites. "On the whole, though," says Stanley Kramer, "they hardly ever left that little house on George Cukor's property. I couldn't help continuing to marvel at how this extraordinary woman had completely given up her own career for Spence."

Kramer also could not help continuing to worry

about Spence.

"He was spending too much time feeling sorry for himself," says Kramer. "I saw him quite a bit—we had a mutual admiration society going —and I honestly do not think he was as sick as he was when we did *Inherit the Wind*. So I said to Kate one day, 'He might just as well work. It's better, for Christ's sake, than his just sitting there with whatever his troubles are.' Kate said, 'Well, who's going to work with him—and in what?' I didn't have an answer then."

But Kramer did have an answer, not long after that. He had gone to Columbia Pictures to do "Andersonville," but the budget got too high and they had to cancel the picture.

"They wanted me to come up with a substitute film, and the idea for it came about while I was walking with William Rose one evening in Beverly Hills. Now, Bill Rose is a good comedy writer. Remember, he did *Mad, Mad World* with me. Anyway, as we walked, he told me a story, to be mostly comedy, about a white South African man, a liberal, whose daughter falls in love with a black guy. I said, 'Geez, we ought to set the story here, in this country, in this background.' I thought of what a sorry joke that was, a liberal father, and later the people thought it was me, whose daughter says, 'This guy I'm in love with is black,' and now I'm faced with all the ways I taught her and brought her up. I thought to myself, 'What a sorry sight to see a front-line liberal come face to face with all his principles right in his own house.' I also thought, 'What a perfect situation for a picture for Tracy.' "

Kramer went to see Tracy and Hepburn when Rose's script for *Guess Who's Coming to Dinner* was still just an idea. Says Kramer,

"I didn't think automatically of Kate for the picture then. I didn't know whether she wanted to work. I was thinking only of Spence. He said, 'I don't want to do it.' I said, 'You should be playing this role. What do you want me to do, get Freddie March, or somebody?' Kate said, 'Spencuh, you should make this picture,' and she amazed me by adding, 'and I'll play your wife.' He grumbled and he said, as he had three times before on my films with him, 'But I get tired, you know.' I said, 'You won't get tired. I'll send you home every day at one in the afternoon. I'll fix it so the studio will never know.' He said, 'Well, OK.' Kate was grinning and clapping her hands silently behind his back."

Playing the old Hollywood game, Kramer then flew to New York to see Sidney Poitier. Kramer says,

"I told Sidney I had no script but that I did have Tracy and Hepburn. Sidney already was a star at that point, but he said, 'I don't know if you can bring it off with the studio, but I'll tell you I'll do it. Absolutely.' So I had three stars committed in heart and principle before I had a word of dialogue on paper. It's a tribute to Kate, Spence and Sidney that Columbia went along. As Spence said to me later, 'Aw, you know, everyone knocks message pictures. Let me tell you something. They don't object to message pictures, nor does the audience. They object to message pictures *that don't make money*. There's a difference.' "

So Rose went to work on the script of *Guess Who's Coming to Dinner,* and when he was finished, everyone liked it. Kramer says, "Columbia liked it because until we reached the short hairs at the end, the story was mostly comedy, but they were still worried about how it would play in the South." Production was set for January 1967.

Then came an unexpected problem, with a

highly unusual solution. Every film production must carry insurance for its stars, so that if a star dies or is incapacitated, there will be enough money to replace him to continue — or to re-do the picture. Kramer says,

"You're never examined for insurance until a few weeks before a picture starts. With all his drinking and ailments, Tracy always qualified for insurance before, so nobody thought it would be a problem in this case. But it was. We couldn't get insurance for Spence. The situation looked desperate. So then we figured out a way of handling it. Kate and I put up *our own salaries* to compensate for the lack of an insurance company for Spence. And we were allowed to proceed."

A short time after that, Abby Mann had a peculiar conversation with Kate Hepburn. Mann says,

"I left my house one morning, rumpled and dishevelled, and started walking down to Santa Monica Boulevard to get some breakfast. I heard someone honking at me from a car. I looked up, and there was Kate. She asked me to climb in and talk with her for a few minutes. I did, and she started the conversation by telling me how much she had liked Oskar Werner and Simone Signoret when she had seen *Ship of Fools*. Then she abruptly changed the subject. She said, 'I'm very upset about Spence. He really, really is worried about dying.' I tried to reassure her by saying how much better he seemed to me, but she continued, 'I come from a doctor's family and dying doesn't mean anything to me, but Spence is really frantic about it. He thinks he's going to die.' Then, the strong lady that she is, she pulled herself together and told me to go off and have my breakfast. And that was that."

When filming began, Tracy seemed better. He was undoubtedly stimulated by working with Kate again, for the first time since *Desk Set*, more than a decade before. He also got tremendous excitement out of his scenes with Sidney Poitier, commenting frequently on what a fine young actor Poitier was. Poitier, in turn, commented frequently on how overwhelmed he was at being in a film with both Tracy and Hepburn, to whom he referred as "giants." Tracy exhibited special interest in the role played by Cecil Kellaway, and he watched intently every time Kellaway was working on-camera. Kellaway's role was that of a Catholic priest, Monsignor Ryan, who advised Matt Drayton, the distraught father (Tracy), about contending with his own life-long liberal principles in the matter of his daughter planning to marry a black man.

True to Kramer's promise, Tracy's work-load was extremely light. He never went beyond lunch-time, and some days he did not work at all. Says Kramer, "I even used a double for most of Spence's over-the-shoulder shots, so that he didn't have to stand around in the many scenes when I didn't have to have the camera on him, full-face. As a result, I think he was much less weak than he had been in either *Inherit the Wind* and *Mad, Mad World*."

Throughout the production, many of the facets of the old Tracy, the teaser, the curmudgeon, were evident. For example, Kramer's wife, Karen, was pregnant, and Tracy kept saying that the baby would be a boy, and that, of course, the Kramers would name him Spencer. Kramer says, "As it turned out, it was a girl, and Karen and I thought it would be nice to name her Katharine, see? Which we did, with an 'a' — Katharine with an 'a'. And Katharine Hepburn, Katharine with an 'a', was her godmother."

Tracy pretended to be enraged, or *was* enraged. Kramer chooses to think it was pretence. He says, "Spence put on his usual act, grousing and saying, 'You promised to name him Spencer. Now name *her* Spencer.' He wanted the little girl to be called Spencer. But when it became Katharine with an 'a', he seemed really pleased enough that that's how the child was named. A little thing, perhaps, but so typical of Spence."

Kramer recalls Tracy's crankiness with Hepburn on this picture. As usual, he alternated lovingness with irritation in his dealings with her on the set.

"I remember one scene they did together," says Kramer, "in which she walked in, when we rehearsed it, and she kneeled down. That was one of the things she knew as a pro: if you get down low, the camera can't see the lines in your face. She did that kneeling quite a bit when it didn't make any difference to the playing of the scene, but this time, it really teed Spence off. He said, 'What the hell are you doing now?' She said, 'Spencuh, I just thought . . .' And he said, 'Spencuh, I just thought . . .', imitating her Bryn Mawr accent and making fun of it. He said, 'Go out, and come in like a human being, for Christ's sake.' Kate just said, 'All right'. She wouldn't take that from anyone else in the whole world. But again, it was so typical of Spence who, a couple of minutes later, would be treating her with great tenderness."

Even more pertinently typical of Tracy was his performance in the crashing finale of *Guess Who's Coming to Dinner*. First, his character, Matt Drayton, goes out into his garden alone, and changes his mind about his daughter marrying a black man, after having been against it through most of the picture. Kramer says, "It's a very contrived scene. But, walking in the garden and changing his mind, Spence carries the entire audience with him. He does it with his face. Who else but Spencer Tracy could have accomplished that with his face."

Then comes the scene in which he confronts everybody, including Poitier's black parents, who also objected to the marriage, and explains why *he* no longer objects. Kramer says he shot the scene in three mornings, three hours per morning, in order not to sap Tracy's strength. Says Kramer,

"I never intended that there would be a counterpart identification with Spence and Kate's real life situation, but it came out that way in this scene. Spence turned to Poitier and said, 'You have to get married, because if you love *her* the way I love her . . .' looking directly at Kate. And Kate burst into tears, and Spence had tears, and so did I. That unintended personal identification made it a scene of fantastic power."

(Later, many critics agreed about the power and poignancy of the scene, vis-a-vis the real life Tracy and Hepburn. Brendan Gill wrote in *The New Yorker* "When, at its climax, Mr. Tracy turns to Miss Hepburn and tells her what an old man remembers, having loved, it is, for us who are permitted to overhear him, an experience that transcends the theatrical." Wanda Hale wrote, "What Tracy says brings tears to the audience, for they feel he is talking about himself as well as the man he is portraying.")

When the very difficult scene was finished, there still were four days of filming to be completed. Kramer says,

"Spence put his arm around me and said, 'You know, I read the script again last night, and if I were to die on the way home tonight, you can still release the picture with what you've got.' He did finish, going away, in very high spirits, causing Sidney Poitier to remark, "He's thriving on this picture; I'm sure of that." When Kramer wound up production on 26 May, Tracy was too tired to go to the "wrap party" for the cast and crew, but he was at home, joyfully calling all his friends and announcing, "I finished it. By God, I finished it."

Suffice it to say, the film, despite Columbia's fears, made a lot of money at the box-office, more than any Tracy *or* Kramer picture in years. Tracy received his ninth Oscar nomination. Hepburn *won* the Oscar for Best Actress, her first since *Morning Glory,* some thirty-four years before.

In thanking Kramer at the end of production, Tracy had been his typical curmudgeon self. As Kramer tells it, "Spence put his tongue in the corner of his mouth, as he always did when he was cynical or amused, and he said, 'Well, Stanley, you've had me doing it against the Bible, and for the Jews, and now for the blacks. What the hell is next?' "

Chapter Thirty

There was to be no next.

Early in the morning of 10 June 1967, just fifteen days after he finished work in *Guess Who's Coming to Dinner,* Tracy was alone in the little rented house on George Cukor's property. It is not clear why he was alone, but Kate Hepburn was not there when the housekeeper, Ida Gheczy, found him shortly before 6 a.m. Some accounts say that he was slumped over the kitchen table with a glass of milk beside him, indicating that his chronic insomnia had caused him to try the old remedy of warm milk for sleeplessness. The official accounts, released to the newspapers for the obituary pages, simply state, as did the *New York Times* in a very rare page one obituary for an actor, that "he was stricken with a heart attack at 6 a.m. and died before the family physician arrived with Carroll Tracy, his brother."

The physician was Dr. Mitchell Covel. It is not

known whether it was he who made the diagnosis of "massive heart attack." There was no autopsy.

But even in his death, there was mystery. Stanley Kramer downplays the heart-attack diagnosis, saying, "Spence really died of gradual deterioration." Also, Kate Hepburn gives a startlingly different time-table for the death, in an article which she wrote for *TV Guide* in March 1986. Speaking about the tireless engine inside Tracy, she wrote: "The engine stopped at *three* one morning. It was June 10, 1967. It just stopped—bang! The box broke. The container had just become too small for all that—what would you call it?—all that wild stuff whirling around inside."

If it happened at 3 a.m. instead of at 6 a.m., was "My Kate" with him at the moment when he finally found peace? It would be comforting to think so.

In the official accounts run by the newspapers, the first to arrive at the St. Ives house, after Carroll and the doctors, were Louise Tracy and their children, John and Susie. Next, at about 11 a.m., came Katharine Hepburn, with George Cukor and Tracy's business manager, Ross Evans.

The Hollywood community mourned, but, for the most part, people were still unaware of the long battle for sobriety which Tracy had waged since he was a young man. They knew only what they read in the newspapers, that he "had suffered a series of ailments since he was stricken with a lung congestion in July 1963, while preparing for a picture with

Miss Hepburn." (There was, of course, no picture with Hepburn at the time. The Hollywood cover-up PR machine was still working.)

The funeral was held at the Immaculate Heart of Mary Catholic Church in Hollywood. The low requiem mass was said by Monsignor O'Donnell, Tracy's priest friend dating back to the *Boys Town* days. Stanley Kramer, one of the pallbearers, says, "I was in the rear of the half-empty church, and, up in the front, during the mass, I saw a man who I guess was so overcome that he fell out of his pew and sprawled in the aisle, before scrambling back into his seat again. Spence would have liked that. It could have been a scene from *It's a Mad, Mad, Mad, Mad World.*"

The funeral, like so much of Tracy's life, had several ironies to it. Louise Tracy was accompanied by Howard Strickling, Tracy's old public relations keeper at MGM. It is said that Strickling stage-managed the entire funeral, strictly limiting attendance to less than six hundred, with the aid of a corps of security guards.

Another irony: Kate Hepburn did not attend the funeral. George Cukor said, "Such a lady. She didn't want to infringe on Louise Tracy at such a time. But believe me, Kate was devastated, really devastated. She had lost the one human being who had been the cornerstone of her life for twenty-five years."

Stanley Kramer went up to the St. Ives house to

see Kate on the night of the funeral. Says Kramer. "She was numb. Vincente Minnelli, the director, was there. He was the guy who always used to amuse Spence by coming up and telling them all the Hollywood gossip, which Spence loved to hear: who was seen at Ciro's with whom, who was screwing whom. But now, Vincente, like the rest of us, just sat there quietly, trying to console Kate."

The next day, Hepburn went back to the seclusion of her family in Connecticut.

After a few weeks, she returned to work—for only the second time in eight years. She wanted to keep busy, she obviously wanted to be the strong woman, trying to overcome her trauma, without forgetting.

The following March, she won her third Oscar for *The Lion in Winter*. Like Tracy, she had come up with two statues in consecutive years.

Still mourning, she spoke as if Tracy were still alive.

"Spencer will be very, very pleased," she said.

Chapter Thirty-one

It is the Spring of 1986.

Louise Tracy has died. She passed away on 13 November 1983. She was eighty-seven years old and laden with honours for her work with the handicapped.

John Tracy, a long-time victim of stroke and other illnesses, is living in a nursing home in California.

Susie, an accomplished photographer and writer, has become an active replacement for her mother on the Board of Directors of the John Tracy Clinic.

The indomitable Kate Hepburn is seventy-seven years old and still rolling along. She has just done her TV drama, Mrs. Delafield Wants to Marry *(for which she receives an Emmy nomination) and she has much other work in her schedule.*

On 10 March 1986, she makes public in the PBS television retrospective THE SPENCER TRACY

LEGACY: A TRIBUTE BY KATHARINE HEPBURN *produced by WNET/New York in association with MGM/VA Television, her remarkable, poignant, revealing open letter to her long-dead great love, Spencer Tracy, in which she captures the truth about the great star's talent, as the following excerpt shows:*

You were really the greatest movie actor. I say this because I believe it and I've heard so many people of standing in our business say it — from Olivier to Lee Strasberg, David Lean, name it. You could do it, and you could do it with that glorious simplicity, that directness. You could just . . . do it.

Chapter Thirty-two

And so, much of the mystery of Tracy's life remains unsolved in the minds of those who knew and loved him best.

His will was a puzzle. He left everything to Louise and his children, with only his clothes, his paintings and his automobiles going to his brother, Carroll. Katharine Hepburn was not mentioned. She kept his old hat.

The attitude of MGM, after his death, was a puzzle, too. Tracy had made hundreds of millions of dollars for the studio throughout his long career with Metro, yet no memorial was ever erected to him. Almost as an afterthought, a small, decrepit office building, deep within the vast expanse of the lot, was eventually named the Tracy Building. It houses the offices of a series for television, which Tracy loathed. Sylvester Stallone has a bigger and more elaborate building named after him.

Needlessly dead at sixty-seven, Tracy left behind the most stubborn mystery of all, the questions still being asked by Hepburn and others. What were the contending forces within him that drove him to acting greatness, but also into his headlong urge for self-destruction?

What *was* it, Spence?, as Kate consistently asks.

And why did he keep everyone at arm's length—even her? Was it to prevent anyone from finding out *why* he was the way he was? Jekyll and Hyde?

So it all remained locked within him, and him alone.

As Hepburn recently said, "He was like an old lion appearing out of the bush, glancing here, glancing there, walking alone in the jungle."

Appendix

Spencer Tracy's Films

Date of Release	Studio	Title	Co-starring	Director
1930	Fox	Up the River	Humphrey Bogart, Claire Luce	John Ford
1931	Fox	Quick Millions	Sally Eilers	Rowland Brown
1931	Fox	Six Cylinder Love	Edward Everett Horton	Thornton Freeland
1931	Fox	Goldie	Jean Harlow	Benjamin Stoloff
1932	Fox	She Wanted a Millionaire	Joan Bennett	John Blyston
1932	United Artists	Sky Devils	William Boyd, Ann Dvorak	Edward Sutherland
1932	Fox	Disorderly Conduct	Sally Eilers, Ralph Bellamy	John W. Considine
1932	Fox	Young America	Doris Kenyon, Ralph Bellamy	Frank Borzage
1932	Fox	Society Girl	James Dunn, Peggy Shannon	Sidney Lanfield

Date of Release	Studio	Title	Co-starring	Director
1932	Fox	*The Painted Woman*	William Boyd, Peggy Shannon	John Blystone
1932	Fox	*Me and My Gal*	Joan Bennett	Raoul Walsh
1932	Warner-First National	*20,000 Years in Sing Sing*	Bette Davis, Lyle Talbot	Michael Curtiz
1933	Fox	*Face in the Sky*	Marian Nixon, Stuart Erwin	Harry Lachman
1933	Fox	*Shanghai Madness*	Fay Wray, Ralph Morgan	John Blystone
1933	Fox	*The Power and the Glory*	Colleen Moore, Ralph Morgan	William K. Howard
1933	Fox	*The Mad Game*	Claire Trevor, Ralph Morgan	Irving Cummings
1933	Columbia	*A Man's Castle*	Loretta Young	Frank Borzage
1934	20th Century	*Looking for Trouble*	Jack Oakie	William Wellman
1934	MGM	*The Show-Off*	Madge Evans	Charles F. Riesner
1934	Fox	*Bottoms Up*	John Boles, Thelma Todd	David Butler

336

1934	Fox	*Now I'll Tell*	Helen Twelvetrees, Alice Faye	Edwin Burke
1934	Fox	*Marie Galante*	Ketti Gallian, Ned Sparks	Henry King
1935	Fox	*It's a Small World*	Wendy Barrie	Irving Cummings
1935	MGM	*The Murder Man*	Virginia Bruce, Lionel Atwell	Tim Whelan
1935	Fox	*Dante's Inferno*	Claire Trevor	Harry Lachman
1935	MGM	*Whipsaw*	Myrna Loy	Sam Wood
1936	MGM	*Riffraff*	Jean Harlow	J. Walter Ruben
1936	MGM	*Fury*	Sylvia Sidney, Walter Abel	Fritz Lang
1936	MGM	*San Francisco*	Clark Gable, Jeanette MacDonald	W.S. Van Dyke
1936	MGM	*Libeled Lady*	Jean Harlow, William Powell, Myrna Loy	Jack Conway
1937	MGM	*They Gave Him a Gun*	Franchot Tone, Gladys George	W.S. Van Dyke
1937	MGM	*Captains Courageous*	Freddie Bartholomew, Lionel Barrymore	Victor Fleming
1937	MGM	*Big City*	Luise Rainer	Frank Borzage
1938	MGM	*Mannequin*	Joan Crawford	Frank Borzage

337

Date of Release	Studio	Title	Co-starring	Director
1938	MGM	Test Pilot	Clark Gable, Myrna Loy	Victor Fleming
1938	MGM	Boys Town	Mickey Rooney	Norman Taurog
1939	20th-Fox	Stanley and Livingstone	Sir Cedric Hardwicke	Henry King
1940	MGM	I Take This Woman	Hedy Lamarr	W.S. Van Dyke
1940	MGM	Northwest Passage	Robert Young	King Vidor
1940	MGM	Edison the Man	Charles Coburn	Clarence Brown
1940	MGM	Boom Town	Clark Gable, Claudette Colbert, Hedy Lamarr	Jack Conway
1941	MGM	Men of Boys Town	Mickey Rooney	Norman Taurog
1941	MGM	Dr. Jekyll and Mr. Hyde	Ingrid Bergman, Lana Turner	Victor Fleming
1942	MGM	Woman of the Year	Katharine Hepburn	George Stevens
1942	MGM	Tortilla Flat	Hedy Lamarr, John Garfield	Victor Fleming
1942	MGM	Keeper of the Flame	Katharine Hepburn	George Cukor
1943	MGM	A Guy Named Joe	Van Johnson, Irene Dunne	Victor Fleming
1944	MGM	The Seventh Cross	Signe Hasso, Hume Cronyn, Jessica Tandy	Fred Zinnemann

1944	MGM	*Thirty Seconds Over Tokyo*	Van Johnson, Robert Walker	Mervyn LeRoy
1945	MGM	*Without Love*	Katharine Hepburn	Harold S. Bucquet
1947	MGM	*The Sea of Grass*	Katharine Hepburn, Melvyn Douglas	Elia Kazan
1947	MGM	*Cass Timberlane*	Lana Turner	George Sidney
1948	MGM	*State of the Union*	Katharine Hepburn, Angela Lansbury, Van Johnson	Frank Capra
1949	MGM	*Edward, My Son*	Deborah Kerr	George Cukor
1949	MGM	*Adam's Rib*	Katharine Hepburn, Judy Holliday	George Cukor
1950	MGM	*Malaya*	James Stewart	Richard Thorpe
1950	MGM	*Father of the Bride*	Elizabeth Taylor, Joan Bennett, Don Taylor	Vincente Minnelli
1951	MGM	*Father's Little Dividend*	Elizabeth Taylor, Joan Bennett, Don Taylor	Vincente Minnelli
1951	MGM	*The People Against O'Hara*	Pat O'Brien, Diana Lynn	John Sturges
1952	MGM	*Pat and Mike*	Katharine Hepburn	George Cukor
1952	MGM	*Plymouth Adventure*	Gene Tierney, Van Johnson	Clarence Brown

Date of Release	Studio	Title	Co-starring	Director
1953	MGM	The Actress	Jean Simmons, Teresa Wright	George Cukor
1954	20th-Fox	Broken Lance	Robert Wagner, Richard Widmark	Edward Dmytryk
1955	MGM	Bad Day at Black Rock	Robert Ryan, Anne Francis, Lee Marvin, Ernest Borgnine	John Sturges
1956	Paramount	The Mountain	Robert Wagner	Edward Dmytryk
1957	20th-Fox	Desk Set	Katharine Hepburn, Joan Blondell, Dina Merrill	Walter Lang
1958	Warner Bros.	The Old Man and the Sea	Felipe Pazes	John Sturges
1958	Columbia	The Last Hurrah	Jeffrey Hunter, Pat O'Brien	John Ford
1960	UA	Inherit the Wind	Fredric March, Gene Kelly	Stanley Kramer
1961	Columbia	The Devil at Four O'Clock	Frank Sinatra	Mervyn LeRoy
1961	UA	Judgment at Nuremberg	Maximilian Schell, Richard Widmark, Burt Lancaster	Stanley Kramer

| 1963 | UA | *It's a Mad, Mad, Mad, Mad World* | Milton Berle, Sid Caesar, Buddy Hackett, Ethel Merman, Mickey Rooney | Stanley Kramer |
| 1967 | Columbia | *Guess Who's Coming to Dinner* | Katharine Hepburn, Sidney Poitier | Stanley Kramer |

Tracy's Academy Award Nominations

1936–As Father Mullin in *San Francisco*
1937–As Manuel in *Captains Courageous* (won the Oscar)
1938–As Father Flanagan in *Boys Town* (won the Oscar)
1950–As Stanley Banks in *Father of the Bride*
1955–As Macreedy in *Bad Day at Black Rock*
1958–As the old man in *The Old Man and the Sea*
1960–As Henry Drummond in *Inherit the Wind*
1961–As Judge Hayward in *Judgment at Nuremberg*
1967–As Matt Drayton in *Guess Who's Coming to Dinner*

Index